WITHOUT LOVE

HE REACTS

THE
CRAZY
CYCLE

SHE REACTS

WITHOUT RESPECT

HIS LOVE

MOTIVATES

THE
ENERGIZING
CYCLE

MOTIVATES

HER RESPECT

HIS LOVE

REGARDLESS OF

THE
REWARDED
CYCLE

REGARDLESS OF

HER RESPECT

Contents

What's the Big Idea?

Welcome! You are about to embark on a wonderful adventure concerning Love and Respect in marriage. As you spend time viewing and discussing the video, you will be answering three major questions.

- Why do we negatively react to each other in marriage? This will be explained in what is called **the Crazy Cycle**.

- How do I best motivate my spouse? **The Energizing Cycle** answers this question.

- What if my spouse does not respond to me? **The Rewarded Cycle** informs us what to do.

A Message From Emerson and Sarah

We are thrilled with your interest and commitment to do this Love and Respect study. Tens of thousands of people have gone through this material which is based on two simple ideas found in Ephesians 5:33: Love and Respect. But the way in which these two interface with each other is profound. When a husband and wife gain insight on Love and Respect, it revolutionizes their marriage. The countless testimonies we have received from individuals and the surveys we have taken of couples confirm this. We want you to believe the same can happen in your relationship. God wants you to believe this! He revealed this truth because He is for you!

About This Study

This is a 10-week DVD study designed to answer the above three questions through video, reflection, devotionals and discussion. Each of the 10 sessions include a video to watch and questions to answer both as a group and for personal reflection. Additionally, there is a short devotional for each person to complete between small group sessions.

Testimony time: Do not underestimate the power of allowing others to share what they have learned and put to work in the "Testimony Time" at the beginning of each session.

Facilitators: The suggestions for application are quite general, but as the group becomes comfortable, encourage them to be more specific so they can clearly assess their progress.

Watch the Video: Sit back, listen, laugh, and watch!

Facilitators: The DVD menu displays 10 sessions, with one video for each week. Following the completion of the video there will be a prompt to guide you into this week's discussion questions. The DVD menu also breaks each session into chapters. These chapters are there to help you go back to a particular section that you may want to review. Go to the main menu, select the appropriate session, and click on the chapter that you would like to review.

In-Session Guide: As you watch the video portion of this study, use this section to take notes and access scripture references. Please note that Emerson's introduction does not include fill in the blanks until later in the first session. All of the answers are located in the back of this guide.

Discussion: There are no trick questions. Most questions ask for an opinion, so have fun sharing your thoughts.

Facilitators: Because of the varying lengths of time that groups meet (some have twenty minutes for discussion and others sixty minutes), not all the questions can be answered during the group discussion time. Therefore, in each session an * is put by a few questions that Emerson feels everyone should answer.

If you have more time, use your discretion as the facilitator in selecting other questions. Be sure to encourage the group to answer the remaining questions on their own during the week. Most questions correlate with the video segment.

Immediate Application: After each session, write down 1-2 things that come to mind during the session that you can apply or practice in the coming week.

Facilitators: Help the group think in terms of practical application. Be sure to stress the importance of writing down thoughts for this section. Encourage them to be prepared (if they feel comfortable) to share how it went at the beginning of the next session.

Mid-week Devotional: In between sessions, there is a mid-week devotional for everyone to read on their own that is related to the topic of the most recently discussed video. It is NOT intended to be read through quickly as part of last-minute preparations for the next session. Instead, the devotional provides an opportunity for everyone to reinforce an idea from the previous session and to spend time away from the group thinking about and applying the Love and Respect principles.

Facilitators: Please strongly encourage everyone to visit this devotional two or three days after your meeting.

Doing This Study Alone Without Your Spouse

Good for you for wanting to learn, grow and be introspective. This study is an incredible way to dig deeper into a topic and is excellent for an individual, couple or group.

Since there may be no one to join you at this time, try your best to bring up the topics you're thinking about with people in your life. Of course, be sensitive if your spouse resists talking. Instead focus on applying the message without talking.

Doing This Study as a Couple

Go through the sections and discussion questions together or do them separately and review together. While doing this, trust each other's goodwill.

If the study becomes challenging to do together - ask questions and seek wisdom from others - perhaps an older, wiser couple who have walked the road in front you, a pastor, or a Christian counselor.

Doing This Study as a Single/Dating Person

We welcome all singles to the Love and Respect Small Group! We believe this message is as relevant to singles as it is to those who are married. The principles learned in this study will help you understand gender differences and how to apply this insight to all of your relationships. For those of you who will eventually marry, the Love and Respect principles applied to your life now will powerfully influence your process of choosing a future spouse, potentially saving you from years of unnecessary heartache.

In most groups, you will be going through this material with married couples as well as singles. Many of the examples and questions are directed to those who are married, but can be easily adapted to other relationships such as the following:

- Friendships
- Dating relationships
- Future marriage
- Parent and sibling relationships
- Work relationships

We encourage you to look for tangible ways to apply what you learn each week to all of your relationships. During the week reflect, pray, and journal on these principles and come prepared to share your discoveries. The goal is to process your thoughts and insights with others in the group, whether they are married or single. We believe strongly that both groups can learn from one another. Our desire is that sharing together will create mutual growth and accountability.

Leading This Study

Thank you! We are grateful to those of you who are willing to answer God's call and lead other couples through this study in order to strengthen their marriages. Our prayer is that your own marriage will be strengthened and blessed in ways beyond your hopes and expectations. We've worked hard to make this study easy to follow and easy for you to lead. As you prepare to facilitate over the next ten weeks, here are a few thoughts to keep in mind.

1. **Don't do it alone.** Pray and ask God to help and guide you throughout the entire study. This is a big responsibility, but God doesn't expect you to do it alone. God promises to equip you for what he has called you to do. He wants you to not only be a blessing to others as you serve, but to also be blessed. Be sure to set aside quiet time with God to allow him to strengthen and encourage you in your own marriage. The foundation of your leadership will come from who you are as a person and your relationship with God.

2. **Be yourself.** You don't need to be an expert! God wants you to use your unique gifts, talents and life experiences. Whether you are an experienced small group leader, or this is your first time, God is pleased with your commitment and will meet you right where you are. Don't worry if you don't always have an answer to a question or you make a mistake. Your group will appreciate your honesty and your efforts, and will love you for it.

3. **Check your leadership style.** Facilitating a group is a big responsibility, but nothing you can't handle. Keep in mind the spouses in your group represent marriages in different circumstances and stages, some strong, others weak. As you lead your group, seek to:

   - **Be relaxed and casual**, but organized and able to keep things moving. Let people share, give opinions, and even disagree a bit, but don't be afraid to sum things up and move to the next question or topic.

   - **Be caring and sensitive.** Some couples in your group might see a lot of humor in certain topics and questions. Others may be hurting and unhappy, not seeing the humor at all. As you go through the study, be aware of those couples who may need a little more guidance and encouragement than others. Some may even want to meet with you in order to talk and pray outside the group. If you feel their issues are beyond your wisdom, don't hesitate to refer them to your pastor or a Christian counselor. *(Also take note: Don't get distracted in your discussions by someone asking about abuse. It's assumed that basic goodwill exists among spouses in this group. If someone is in harm's way, they need to speak privately with someone in leadership and seek help from those in authority.)*

- **Be accepting and non-threatening**. For example, if someone comes up with an opinion that is totally counter to what Emerson sometimes refers to as "typical" or "generally speaking," do not be defensive or argumentative. Let everyone give opinions, then sum up by saying,

    "According to Emerson's extensive experience and research on marital communication, this is what he sees to be the norm or what is typical of men and women, husband and wives. He knows there are exceptions to any 'general rule,' but he has also found that regardless of how people think or act, they all need Love and Respect in communication."

- **Be an encourager.** Encourage the couples in your group to attend every session, engage fully in the discussion, pray and complete each session in their workbook. Help them to see God working in them and in their marriage relationship throughout the study. As you lead, be sensitive to personality types (i.e.introvert and extrovert). Gently draw out the quieter members by asking non-threatening questions such as, "What do you think about this?" Encourage talkative members to fully share but not dominate the discussion. Never allow unsolicited advice.

4. **Prepare for your meeting ahead of time**. It is best to review the video session and the study guide for that session ahead of time. This will allow you to be better prepared for leading the discussions and also familiarize you with the exercises at the end of each session.

5. **Depend on God's leading**. Prayer should be an important part of every meeting. Feel free to pray and lead your group with your own prayer or have someone else in the group lead in prayer. It is also important to pray for the couples in your group throughout the study.

6. **Session timing.** Do your best to honor the time frame you have planned for each week. People will appreciate being able to depend on your group time starting and ending on time. Emerson spends the majority of the first session talking before any fill in the blanks, so encourage participants to just sit back and listen, and perhaps take some notes. Remind your group that all of the answers are in the back of this book.

7. **Verses in the Session Guide**: Because I had the privilege as a pastor-teacher of studying the Bible 30 hours a week for nearly 20 years, I looked at everything in the Bible related to marriage. The concepts that I teach are derived from what the Scriptures reveal. As you go through this content, please read these verses. In the video I will not cover the majority of these. For this reason do not deprive yourself of being blessed by the richness of God's word on marriage. Please read these and be edified. All verses are from the New American Standard Bible (NASB) unless otherwise specified. Also, you will notice some verses are indented. These Scriptures show the exceptions.

Thank You for allowing God to use you by serving as a small group leader. Your willingness and commitment to dedicate your time, effort, and energy is a priceless gift. You are the ones making a difference in the battle against failed marriages and divorce.

May God bless you and your marriage!

- Dr. Emerson and Sarah Eggerichs

In-Session Guide

The Craziness!

Decoding the Craziness!

Research found that _____ and _____ are the two key ingredients for a successful marriage.

Though we all need _____ and _____ equally, the felt need during conflict is as different as female is from male (Matthew 19:4).

His and Her Deepest Value- What Is the Deepest Value or Need?

Each need is most apparent when threatened.

In the Diet Book story she hears, "I don't accept, approve of, or love you unless you look like a Dallas Cowboy Cheerleader."

In the Marriage Book story he hears, "I don't accept, approve of, or respect you unless you change and become more loving like me."

Ephesians 5:33 Nevertheless, each individual among you also is to love his own wife even as himself, and the wife must see to it that she respects her husband.

We asked 7,000 people this question: When you are in a conflict with your spouse or significant other, do you feel unloved at that moment or disrespected?

83% of the _____ said they feel disrespected.

72% of the _____ said they feel unloved.

During conflict, when you see the spirit of your spouse deflate, the issue is no longer the issue! When the issue isn't the issue, what is the issue? We believe that she is feeling _____ and he is feeling _____.

God revealed this truth 2,000 years ago in Ephesians 5:33!

_____

_____

_____

_____

_____

_____

_____

_____

_____

_____

Is This Why Things Get Crazy? Yes.

- Without love she reacts without respect.

- Without respect he reacts without love.

Colossians 3:19 Husbands, love your wives ...

1 Peter 3:1-2 ... even if any of them are disobedient to the Word, they may be won without a word by the behavior of their wives, as they observe your... respectful behavior.

Are You Sure Love and Respect Are These Deepest Needs?

Science and Scripture reveal the code about the two deepest values.

Genesis 29:32 ... surely now my husband will love me.

Judges 16:15 How can you say, "I love you," when your heart is not with me?

2 Samuel 6:16-22 ... Michal ... saw ... David ... dancing before the Lord; and she despised him in her heart ... David said ... "I will be more lightly esteemed ..."

Is She Conscious of Her Need for Love and Is He Conscious of His Need for Respect?

Many gals wonder, "Does he love me as much as I love him?"

Many guys simmer, "I get no respect."

Genesis 29:32-33 Leah ... said ... "the Lord has heard that I am unloved ..."

Judges 14:16 Samson's wife wept ... and said, "You only hate me, and you do not love me."

Esther 1:17 ... to look with contempt on their husbands ...

Esther 1:20 ... then all women will give honor to their husbands, great and small.

Hosea 2:14 ... I will allure her ... and speak kindly ["tenderly," NIV] to her.

Proverbs 2:16 ... the adulteress who flatters with her words.

_____

_____

_____

_____

_____

_____

_____

_____

Why Do We Hear More About Love in Marriage Than Respect?

Research shows that women are more expressive-responsive in marriage.

In today's love-dominated society, a woman tends to talk far more about her need for love than her husband speaks about his need for respect.

We need to think biblically, not just culturally. Biblically there are two sides to the marital coin: love AND respect. Though Paul penned the Love Chapter (1 Corinthians 13) and Peter walked with the Lord of Love for three years, neither command a wife to agape-love her husband.

Only the husband is commanded to agape-love his wife (Ephesians 5:25, 28, 33).

Both Peter and Paul reveal that the secret for a wife is to show unconditional respect (1 Peter 3:1-2; Ephesians 5:33). This empowers her.

Though it seems counter-intuitive and counter-cultural, unconditional respect is as powerful to a husband as unconditional love is to a wife. This truth needs to be put back on the marital radar screen.

The Misunderstanding About Respect

Isn't the Opposite True: Gals Need R-E-S-P-E-C-T and Guys Need L-O-V-E?

- We all need love and respect equally. However during conflict, a wife leans toward love and a husband toward respect.
- When a wife requests R-E-S-P-E-C-T, often she desires to be treated and honored as an equal (1 Peter 3:7). Feeling like a second-class citizen (on par with a doormat) sends her through the roof!
- When a husband wishes to feel L-O-V-E between them, it revolves around her liking him as a friend. He does not feel the love between them when she is unfriendly and negative (Titus 2:4).

Titus 2:4 Encourage the young women to love ["phileo," not "agape"] their husbands …

1 Peter 3:7 Husbands … grant her honor [the Greek word means "valuing"] as a fellow heir of the grace of life …

Ephesians 5:33 … love his own wife … and the wife must see to it that she respects her husband.

_____

_____

_____

_____

_____

_____

_____

_____

_____

Isn't it Agreed That Love Is the Most Important Ingredient and Respect Is Marginal?

What is your read on this phrase: GODISNOWHERE? An atheist might see "God is nowhere." A believer might see "God is now here." In other words, what one deeply believes will affect the way one interprets life.

Her pink lenses see love and his blue lenses see respect. Neither are wrong, just different.

When the Bible says that love is the greatest of these (1 Corinthians 13:13), Paul is comparing love to faith and hope, not to respect (Ephesians 5:33). We must accurately handle the word of truth (2 Timothy 2:15).

God made us male and female. Thus, a husband is not wrong for needing respect, just different from his wife. A wife is not wrong for needing love, just different from her husband. A wise person sees these differences and celebrates them.

Genesis 1:27 And God created man in His own image, in the image of God He created him; male and female He created them.

Matthew 19:4 Have you not read, that He who created [them] from the beginning made them male and female?

1 Peter 3:7 … since she is a woman …

1 Thessalonians 2:7 … As a nursing mother tenderly cares for her own children.

Isaiah 54:6 Like a wife forsaken and grieved in spirit … like a wife … when she is rejected …

Jeremiah 30:6 Ask now, and see, if a male can give birth …

1 Corinthians 16:13 … act like men, be strong.

Nehemiah 4:14 … fight for … your wives …

1 Peter 3:7 Husbands … live with your wives in an understanding way … since she is a woman …

Proverbs 19:14 … a prudent wife …

Don't Some Wives Feel Uncomfortable Showing Respect to a Husband?

Some contend showing respect makes a husband superior and a wife inferior. However, the Bible is clear: in the eyes of God a husband and wife are equal.

_____

_____

_____

_____

_____

_____

_____

_____

As for a wife's feelings of discomfort, a wife need not feel respect in order to show respect. And, showing respect does not mean giving a husband license to do whatever he desires. Peter, who teaches unconditional respect, watched the wife of Anania--her name was Sapphira--drop dead because she went along with her husband in lying to God (Acts 5:1-11). A wife needs to respectfully take a stand. Unconditional respect means, "There is no condition, circumstance, or situation that can get me to show contempt to my husband."

Unconditional respect means a wife gives the gift of a respectful demeanor when confronting a husband's wrong behavior. This is about who she is, not about who he isn't.

Galatians 3:28 There is neither male nor female; for you are all one in Christ Jesus.

1 Peter 3:7 Husbands ... grant her honor as a fellow heir of the grace of life ...

1 Corinthians 7:4 The wife does not have authority over her own body, but the husband does; and likewise also the husband does not have authority over his own body, but the wife does.

1 Corinthians 11:11 ... in the Lord, neither is woman independent of man, nor is man independent of woman.

1 Samuel 18:20f; 6:16f Michal ... loved David ... Then ... Michal despised him in her heart ...

1 Titus 3:11 Women likewise must be dignified ...

Proverbs 31:25 ... dignity ... her clothing ...

What if a Husband Doesn't Deserve Respect?

- When he fails to love as he ought, he doesn't deserve respect. However, this isn't about him deserving respect but about him needing respect.
- By way of analogy, Hosea the prophet was to win his adulterous wife by loving her. She was neither lovable nor deserving, but she needed love.
- Similarly, Peter instructs wives to win a disobedient husband through respectful behavior. A disobedient husband is neither respectable nor deserving, but contempt will not win him. To win a husband, a wife cannot show disdain any more than a husband can show hostility to win a wife.
- Sadly, because the culture teaches that respect must be earned (whereas love is to be unconditional), women have been given license to express, "I love you but don't respect you." However, that's comparable to a husband declaring, "I respect you but do not love you."

_____

_____

_____

_____

_____

_____

_____

_____

_____

Luke 6:32 And if you love those who love you, what credit is that to you?

Hosea 3:1 Go again, love a woman who is loved by her husband, yet an adulteress …

1 Peter 3:1-2 Even if any of them are disobedient to the word, they may be won without a word by the behavior of their wives, as they observe your … respectful behavior.

Are You Saying He Needs Unconditional Respect Equal to Her Need for Unconditional Love?

- Like needing oxygen, she needs unconditional love and he needs unconditional respect. Both have equal needs though these needs are not the same.
- Unconditional love means there is no circumstance that can get a husband to show hostility toward his wife. That's his dogged decision. She does not make him harsh and hostile but reveals these things about him.
- Unconditional respect means there is no situation that can get a wife to be derisive. That's her weapon of choice.
- Unconditional respect is a biblical teaching.

1 Peter 2:17 Honor all men; love the brotherhood … honor the king.

1 Peter 2:18 … respect … those who are good and gentle, but also… those who are unreasonable.

Romans 12:10 Be devoted to one another in brotherly love; give preference to one another in honor.

_____
_____
_____
_____
_____
_____
_____
_____
_____
_____
_____
_____
_____
_____
_____
_____
_____

Discussion Questions

1. God's Last Word to the Church on Marriage

If my father is on his deathbed and says, "Emerson come close and listen to me," you know his last words are his most important words. You might say that God's last word to the church on marriage is Ephesians 5:33. This is His summary statement! Though God isn't dying, the significance of this revelation is to be heeded. There you read that husbands must love their wives and wives must respect their husbands.

Is this a divine suggestion or a divine command? Explain.

WE MUST do IT

2. The Need*

How does Ephesians 5:33 suggest a wife needs her husband's love and a husband needs his wife's respect? NATURLEY Loveing A-d Respected

3. The Differences*

Because God made you male and female, is it okay that your spouse has a need that you don't have? Explain.

Please say out loud this phrase: "Not wrong, just different." Remember, the color blue is not wrong because it is different from the color pink!

4. Pink and Blue

Many couples find the pink and blue analogy helpful. A wife looks at the world through pink sunglasses, listens through pink hearing aids, and speaks through a pink megaphone. A husband sees through blue sunglasses, hears through blue hearing aids, and talks through a blue megaphone. For instance, Emerson uses the example of what a woman means when she says through her pink megaphone, "I have nothing to wear" versus what a husband means when saying through his blue megaphone, "I have nothing to wear."

How does this example reinforce the idea that you are not wrong, just different?

_____

_____

_____

_____

_____

_____

_____

_____

5. Blue's Emotions and Pink's Sexuality

Because of the husband's blue nature, why would a husband not have fond feelings of love and affection in his heart toward a wife he thinks despises who he is as a human being? In other words, why would he tend to move away from her instead of wanting to emotionally connect with her?

Because of the wife's pink nature, why would she not be sexually responsive to a husband who is harsh and angry with her? In other words, why would she tend to shut down and pull back on what appears to be hostility?

6. Standing on Air Hoses

Another analogy that helps couples is the air tanks and air hoses. A wife needs love like she needs air to breathe. She has an air hose connected to her love tank. When her husband stands on her air hose, like an elephant eating peanuts, she tends to react negatively. She is feeling un-loved.

On the other hand, a husband needs respect like he needs air to breathe. He has an air hose connected to his respect tank. When his wife lays down on his air hose, like a fawn with her fawnettes having a picnic, he tends to react negatively. He is feeling disrespected.

What does this word picture say to you?

7. When the Issue Isn't the Issue

When you see the spirit of your spouse deflate, you are stepping on their air hose. Whatever the topic at hand (finances, sex, children, in-laws, etc.), as important as that topic is, when the spirit of your spouse deflates a deeper issue now exists! The issue is no longer the issue! Your wife is feeling unloved and your husband is feeling disrespected.

Up to this point how have you responded to your spouse when his or her spirit deflated and you realized "the issue was no longer the issue"?

8. The Diet Book and the Marriage Book

From the video, can you recall what message the wife heard through her pink hearing aids when her husband gave her the diet book?

_____

_____

_____

_____

_____

_____

_____

_____

_____

Why would she feel disapproved and unaccepted?

When she felt unloved, how did she react?

What message did the husband hear in his blue hearing aids when he saw the third marriage book (this year) next to his recliner?

Why would he feel disapproved and unaccepted?

When he felt disrespected, how did he react?

9. Unconditional Love and Respect

According to Hosea 3:1, what wins the heart of a wife (if anything will) because it meets her deepest need?

According to 1 Peter 3:1–2 (NASB), what wins the heart of a husband (if anything will) because it meets his deepest need?

10. But How Can I Love or Respect Sin?

Explain the difference between Hosea showing love for his wife's adulterous actions and Hosea being a loving man toward her heart while confronting her "unlovable" behaviors. Which was the Lord asking him to do?

Likewise, explain the difference between a wife respecting her husband's disobedient actions and a wife coming across as a respectful woman toward his heart while confronting his "unrespect-able" behaviors. Which is Peter asking her to do?

Imagine saying to your spouse: *"There is nothing you can do to get me to stop loving/respecting the person God sees in you and I see in you! But I love/respect you too much to let you continually give in to this sin."* What do you think would happen?

Remember Jesus' example. He said the spirit is willing but the flesh is weak. He unconditionally loved and respected the spirit of a person while confronting carnal behaviors.

11. Refusing to Believe That God Designed Marital Conflict*

Paul wrote that if two people marry they have not sinned but they will have "trouble" (1 Corinthians 7:28). Did you hear that? God predicts trouble.

_____

_____

_____

_____

_____

_____

_____

_____

_____

For example, earlier Paul reveals that a wife does not have authority over her own body, but the husband does; and the husband does not have authority over his own body; the wife does (1 Corinthians 7:4). This is referring to sexual intimacy. Both have equal say! So, who decides if there will be sexual intimacy tonight? The answer is "yes!" God designed conflict and with that comes trouble! Did you know God's Word teaches this?

What would you say to the person who encounters trouble and interprets that as being outside of God's will? Does trouble mean you have made a mistake in marrying this person?

Immediate Application

Write down in the space below one or two things that came to mind during this session that you already know you need to begin applying or practicing this week.

_____

_____

_____

_____

_____

_____

_____

_____

_____

_____

_____

_____

_____

_____

_____

_____

_____

_____

_____

_____

_____

_____

Midweek Devotional
Pink and Blue: Not Wrong, Just Different

He created them male and female, and He blessed them.

—Genesis 5:2

One of the most powerful and eye-opening concepts in the Love and Respect approach to marriage is the difference between Pink and Blue. We aren't talking about how to decorate a nursery. We are simply pointing out how God made men and women as different as the colors pink and blue. I use the simple analogy that the woman looks at the world through Pink sunglasses that color all she sees. The man, however, looks at the world through Blue sunglasses that color all he sees.

Men and women can look at precisely the same situation and see life very differently. Inevitably, their Pink and Blue lenses cause their interpretation of things to be at odds, in some cases more so than others. Men and women not only see differently, but they also hear differently. To carry the Pink and Blue analogy a little further, God created men with Blue hearing aids and women with Pink hearing aids. They may hear the same words but receive very different messages, as in the statement "I have nothing to wear!" She hears nothing new, while he hears nothing clean.

Because men and women figuratively wear sunglasses and hearing aids in different colors, they see, hear, and behave differently in countless ways: When she wants to talk face-to-face and he wants her to sit next to him and watch football, this is a Pink and Blue difference. When she wants their ten-year-old son to be more careful riding his bike and he wants his boy to ride that bike the way he himself did when he was ten, this is a Pink and Blue difference. When she wants to clean the kitchen, launder the sheets, and vacuum the carpet right away and he wants her to forgo these chores to play with him and the kids, this is a Pink and Blue difference.

Many couples arrive at our conferences suffering from "color blindness" regarding the profound impact the principle of Pink and Blue has on marriage, but when they leave, their color blindness is gone. They make observations like these:

- "I never saw that before. I thought we were the same."
- "Now I understand how men and women are 'wired' differently and why it takes a lot of work to learn about each other's needs."
- "I am able to view conflict totally differently now. Instead of seeing my husband as an egotistical maniac, I have some peace and confidence about who God made me to be and who God made him to be, and I'm not feeling so frustrated about our differences."

Refusing to get frustrated is the key. Genesis 1:27 tells us that God made us in His image, and Genesis 5:2 adds that He blessed what He made. When differences arise (and they always will), remember this is part of God's plan. Neither one of you is wrong, just different. A major step toward a happy marriage is accepting differences and working them out with love and respect. Relax—and even rejoice. "Viva la difference!"

Prayer: Thank the Lord that in the very beginning He created male and female—Blue and Pink. Ask Him for patience and ever-growing understanding of how men and women see and hear differently.

Action: When *the Crazy Cycle* threatens to spin over a Pink and Blue difference of opinion, try saying things like, "Here, put on my Pink sunglasses so you can see what I see," or "Here, try my Blue hearing aids so you can hear what I just heard."

For more "husband-friendly devotionals that wives truly love," see Emerson's book The Love & Respect Experience (Thomas Nelson, 2011).

In-Session Guide

We asked 7,000 people this question: When you are in a conflict with your spouse or significant other, do you feel unloved at that moment or disrespected?

83% of the _____ said they feel disrespected.

72% of the _____ said they feel unloved.

During conflict, when you see the spirit of your spouse deflate, the issue is no longer the issue! When the issue isn't the issue, what is the issue? We believe that she is feeling _____ and he is feeling _____.

God revealed this truth 2,000 years ago in Ephesians 5:33!

Is This Why We React and Things Get a Bit Crazy?

She reacts in ways that feel disrespectful to her husband when feeling _____. He reacts in ways that feel unloving to his wife when feeling _____

This description of *the Crazy Cycle* is not presented so that we can justify our disobedience to Ephesians 5:33.

Proverbs 30:21-23 The earth quakes … under an unloved woman when she gets a husband …

Ezekiel 16:45 … who loathed their husbands …

Genesis 30:1 Now when Rachel saw that she bore Jacob no children, she became jealous of her sister; and she said to Jacob, "Give me children, or else I die."

Genesis 30:2 Then Jacob's anger burned against Rachel, and he said, "Am I in the place of God who has withheld from you the fruit of the womb?"

How Do I Get My Spouse to Meet My Need?

A wife sees her acts of love as respectful and a husband sees his acts of respect as loving. Thus both wonder, "Why should my spouse feel disrespected or unloved?"

_____

_____

_____

_____

_____

_____

_____

_____

_____

However, a wife tends to overlook the demoralizing power of her disrespectful reactions, and a husband is inclined to ignore the devastating power of his unloving reactions.

We have a propensity to see our goodwilled deposits and miss the impact of our negative withdrawals, and then wonder why the marriage borders on emotional bankruptcy.

Proverbs 14:12 There is a way which seems right to a man, but its end is the way of death.

What if He Says, "I Don't Know if I Love You" and She Says, "You Don't Deserve My Respect"?

Ignorantly she said, "You don't deserve my respect." Though she uttered this line, she is trying to awaken her husband to her need to feel his love. Besides, he should know that she doesn't really mean it!

Ignorantly he said, "I don't know if I ever loved you." Though he aired these words, he did not say what he meant. He meant to say, "I don't know if I ever loved you the way you need to be loved." He failed to finish the sentence.

If a spouse did mean what they said, was this a mere snapshot comment at a point in time? If so, we must not hold on to this one-liner as representative of their deepest sentiments. We must look at the whole script to the marital movie.

Proverbs 12:18 There is one who speaks rashly [thoughtlessly] like the thrusts of a sword ...

James 3:2 For we all stumble in many ways. If anyone does not stumble in what he says, he is a perfect man, able to bridle the whole body as well.

Can a Good Marriage Become Better and a Poor Marriage Become Good? Yes!

If goodwill exists, then most conflict is due to a misunderstanding of each person's core value.

Healing comes when both believe in the other's goodwill even though the reactions have felt unloving and disrespectful.

1 Corinthians 7:33 But one who is married is concerned about ... how he may please his wife ... how she may please her husband.

_____

_____

_____

_____

_____

_____

_____

_____

Proverbs 31:11 The heart of her husband trusts in her ...

Proverbs 31:12 She does him good and not evil all the days of her life.

Ecclesiastes 9:9 Enjoy life with the woman whom you love all the days of your fleeting life which He has given to you under the sun; for this is your reward in life ...

1 Corinthians 7:11 ... let her ... be reconciled to her husband.

I Hold My Spouse Responsible (to Blame), So How Do I Get Him/Her to Move First?

The one who sees himself or herself as **the most mature moves first.**

Placing blame isn't the way to go. Put it this way: it won't work when a husband insists, "I will love her only after she starts showing me more respect. After all, she is causing me to be unloving." It is ineffective for a wife to put her heels in and contend, "He must first love me before I will show him any respect! He's to blame for my disrespect."

My Response is My Responsibility! My response is not my spouse's responsibility. Mature people get this!

James 3:13 Who among you is wise ...? Let him show ... his deeds in the gentleness of wisdom.

Matthew 7:24 Therefore everyone who hears these words of Mine, and acts upon them, may be compared to a wise man, who built his house upon the rock.

Genesis 3:12 And the man said, "The woman whom Thou gavest to be with me, she gave me from the tree, and I ate."

Genesis 3:13 Then the Lord God said to the woman, "What is this you have done?" And the woman said, "The serpent deceived me, and I ate."

Proverbs 30:20 This is the way of an adulterous woman: She eats and wipes her mouth, and says, "I have done no wrong."

Malachi 2:15-16 Take heed then, to your spirit, and let no one deal treacherously against the wife of your youth. "For I hate divorce," says the Lord ... So take heed to your spirit ...

What Can I Do When My Immature Spouse Makes Me So Mad?

Your spouse doesn't "make" you mad. What happens during a fight when you feel that you have lost emotional control and the phone rings?

Galatians 5:19-20 The deeds of the flesh are evident, which are ... enmities, strife, jealousy, outbursts of anger, disputes, dissensions, and factions.

What if I Choose to Act on This?

Love empowers a husband to energize his wife.

Respect empowers a wife to energize a husband.

The key to motivating another person is meeting that person's deepest need, especially during conflict. Over time, acting on Ephesians 5:33 increases one's influence and energizes the marriage.

Proverbs 24:5 A wise man is strong, and a man of knowledge increases power.

1 Corinthians 7:16 For how do you know, O wife, whether you will save your husband? Or how do you know, O husband, whether you will save your wife?

Hosea 3:1 The LORD said to me, "Go, show your love to your wife again, though she is loved by another and is an adulteress. Love her as the LORD loves the Israelites" (NIV).

Judges 19:3 Her husband ... went after her to speak tenderly to her ... to bring her back ...

1 Peter 3:1 Even if any of them are disobedient to the word, they may be won without a word by the behavior of their wives, as they observe your ... respectful behavior.

Isn't This Too Simplistic Since So Many Other Problems Exist?

The problems are not the problem; the root issue is an unloving and disrespectful attitude. Though a plethora of issues envelope you (we will have trouble in marriage!) like money problems, in-law struggles, child-rearing frustrations, health concerns, and the list goes on, it is your loving and respectful response to your spouse during these tensions that leads to marital success. It is hostility and contempt that lead to marital failure, not the troubles.

Will we believe the revelation from God that Love and Respect is His final word (so to speak) to the church on what makes a marriage successful?

1 Corinthians 7:28 If you should marry, you have not sinned ... Yet such will have trouble in this life.

Ephesians 5:33 Nevertheless, each individual among you also is to love his own wife even as himself, and the wife must see to it that she respects her husband.

Ephesians 3:3 ... that by revelation there was made known to me ...

2 Peter 3:15-16 ... our beloved brother Paul, according to the wisdom given him, wrote to you, as also in all his letters ... which the untaught and unstable distort, as they do also the rest of the Scriptures, to their own destruction.

Psalm 19:7 The testimony of the Lord is sure, making wise the simple.

Psalm 119:130 The unfolding of Thy words gives light; it gives understanding to the simple.

What Is a Major Mistake Couples Make?

We believe that he can be unloving to get respect and she can be disrespectful to get love.

We cannot use unholy means to achieve worthy ends. We cannot be negative to motivate another person to be positive.

We cannot deprive another person of what they need in order to motivate them to meet our needs.

Colossians 3:19 Husbands, love your wives, and do not be embittered against them.

1 Samuel 25:3 The man's name was Nabal, and his wife's name was Abigail ... the man was harsh and evil in his dealings.

Proverbs 12:4 She who shames him is as rottenness in his bones.

Proverbs 21:19 It is better to live in a desert land, than with a contentious and vexing woman.

Genesis 30:1-2 Now when Rachel saw that she bore Jacob no children ... she said to Jacob, "Give me children, or else I die." Then Jacob's anger burned against Rachel, and he said, "Am I in the place of God, who has withheld from you the fruit of the womb?"

_____
_____
_____
_____
_____
_____
_____
_____
_____

The Love and Respect Connection

There are important definitions and connections between love and respect.

The Crazy Cycle: Why do we negatively react to each other? When she feels unloved, she reacts without respect. When he feels disrespected, he reacts without love.

The Energizing Cycle: How do we motivate a spouse? His love motivates her respect. Her respect motivates his love.

The Rewarded Cycle: What should we do even when a spouse doesn't respond? His love unto Christ blesses regardless of her respect. Her respect unto Christ blesses regardless of his love.

Discussion Questions

For Better, Not Worse: A One-Sentence Success Story

Testimony Time: Several of you state briefly what you applied from the last session.

For example . . .

- While we were having a little spat I kept saying to myself, "My spouse isn't wrong, just different."
- I realized that when the spirit of my spouse deflated, the topic we were talking about was no longer the issue, but this was a love and respect issue.
- This week I said, "That felt disrespectful (or unloving). Did I just come across as unloving (or disrespectful)?"

1. The Crazy Cycle*

Men, when your wife reacts negatively in a conflict, try to explain how that comes across to you as disrespectful.

Women, when your husband reacts negatively in a conflict, try to explain how that comes across to you as unloving.

Do you find yourselves going round and round, with each negative reaction triggering a negative reaction in the other?

2. The Continuum

A wife still needs R.E.S.P.E.C.T. and a husband still needs love. However, why is there not one greeting card from a husband to a wife that says, "Baby, I really respect you"? Alternatively, why during conflicts does a husband not say, "You don't love me" but announces, "I don't deserve this disrespect!"?

How is it that a husband could be assured of his wife's love, yet not feel she likes him as a person?

_____

_____

_____

_____

_____

_____

_____

_____

_____

3. The Command from God

Read Ephesians 5:33.

Since God commands the husband to love his wife, why is he always wrong when saying, "I will not be a loving person when my wife fails to show respect"?

Since God commands the wife to respect her husband, why is she always wrong when saying, "I will not be a respectful person when my husband fails to show love"?

4. Decoding the Code*

Discuss how husbands and wives often send messages to each other "in code" (i.e., what they say is not what they really mean).

For instance, what does a wife mean when she vents, "You never spend any time with me!"? Is she meaning to be disrespectful and condemning, or is she crying out to the man who matters to her the most because she wants to experience the love that only he can give her?

What does a husband mean when he says, "I don't want to talk about it. Drop it"? Is he saying that he does not love his wife? Or, is he saying that he is losing energy in some of these "talks" because it comes around to him being inadequate and he feels disrespected for who he is as a human being?

5. The Wife Who Died*

In the video Emerson told the story of the all-night bus ride. In that story we learn that a father had gotten on the bus with his three children, all of whom were running wild and disturbing the passengers.

Further, the father did nothing to stop them but only stared out the window. With each passing moment the passengers grew livid. But the wrath of the passengers vanished when learning that his wife, their mother, had just died in the hospital. Suddenly the father's behavior made sense. He was in shock, and his kids were acting out since they had never lost a mommy before.

When first observing this father and children, we believe the father is a permissive parent and the children are disobedient. We feel ourselves being "offended."

_____

_____

_____

_____

_____

_____

_____

_____

_____

However, we stop feeling "offended" when the facts come out. This new information enables us to decode. We realize our interpretation was wrong and we quickly feel compassion instead of anger. Did you feel the same? Why or why not?

6. Wrongly Taking Up Offense*

We can also wrongly take up "offense" against our spouse on the marital bus ride.

For example, when your wife receives the diet book from you, she hears a message of disapproval. She feels unloved. She reacts defensively. But here's what happens. Her reaction feels disrespectful to you. You are offended when she shouts, "You men have two brains. One is lost and the other is out looking for it!"

Though you feel offended by her put-down, how can you decode your wife's vulnerability?

Or, when your husband receives the third marriage book from you, he hears a message of disapproval. He feels disrespected and he reacts defensively. But here's what happens. His reaction feels unloving to you. You are offended when he stonewalls and refuses to read the book.

Though you feel offended by his neglect of the marriage, how can you decode your husband's vulnerability?

7. Getting Too Defensive and Thereby Becoming Offensive

As a husband (who refuses to read the marriage book) or wife (who reacts emotionally after getting the diet book), explain how your defensive reactions come across as offensive even if this is not your intention.

What is our responsibility as believers to go the extra mile and not appear offensive (1 Corinthians 10:32)?

If you softened your defensive reactions, how would this stop *the Crazy Cycle*?

8. Judging My Spouse as Childish

We can too easily judge our spouse's weaknesses because where they are vulnerable, God gave us natural strengths. For example, because a husband is not bothered by a diet book (he doesn't

_____
_____
_____
_____
_____
_____
_____
_____

feel unloved when receiving a diet book), he can wrongly judge his wife as childish for feeling unloved and reacting negatively to the diet book.

And, because a wife is not bothered by the third marriage book this year for the two of them to read (she wouldn't feel disrespected if he bought a marriage book), she can wrongly judge her husband as childish for feeling disrespected and reacting negatively to the marriage book.

Explain how *the Crazy Cycle* will slow down if couples stop judging one another in their areas of weakness.

9. Claiming My Spouse Lacks Goodwill

During moments of craziness, a wise person does not impugn motives.

About the diet book: A husband needs to discern that after his wife receives the diet book, she is not seeking to emasculate him, but to awaken him to the longing of her heart to be loved by him. She is not intending to be mean. And, a wife needs to discern that her husband isn't seeking to be condemning and unloving for getting the diet book, but after she complained about being overweight he got the diet book to be helpful. (Every guy makes this mistake once!)

About the marriage book: A wife needs to recognize that after her husband receives the third marriage book this year to read, he is not trying to crush his wife's spirit by ignoring the book, but to alert her to his feelings. He is not intending to be cruel, but is feeling criticized as unacceptable and losing energy in the marriage. And, a husband needs to detect that his wife isn't seeking to be judgmental and disrespectful by giving him the third marriage book, but is trying to be helpful.

When two people give the benefit of the doubt to the other, trusting each other's goodwill, what happens? Why?

10. Disagreeing with What the Bible Says about Good Intentions*

The Bible says that a husband is concerned about how to please his wife and a wife is concerned about how to please her husband (1 Corinthians 7:33–34).

Paul, who penned this line, knew full well about the total depravity of the human heart. God used him to write the book of Romans, which unfolds the sinfulness of humanity! Paul understood that we need the Savior because of our condition.

_____

_____

_____

_____

_____

_____

_____

_____

Yet, in marriage Paul inspires us with the idea that in general a spouse, though sinful and sometimes intentionally nasty, does not intend to be displeasing or unconcerned.

Paul recognized that we can act on the image of God within us, not enough to be redeemed by our good intentions, but enough to want to please a spouse. In other words, Paul assumes basic goodwill in most marriages. Essentially, a wife is not campaigning to show contempt. A husband is not on the march to show hostility.

What does 1 Corinthians 7:33–34 mean to you?

What happens when you conclude your spouse is Hitler's distant cousin?

Discuss what changes within you when you accept that your spouse does not intend evil but is reacting negatively because she feels unloved, or he feels disrespected.

Immediate Application

Write down in the space below one or two things that came to mind during this session that you already know you need to begin applying or practicing this week.

_____

_____

_____

_____

_____

_____

_____

_____

_____

_____

_____

_____

_____

_____

_____

_____

_____

_____

_____

_____

Midweek Devotional
Do You Have a Goodwilled Marriage?

He who seeks good finds goodwill, but evil comes to him who searches for it.

—Proverbs 11:27 NIV

I am sometimes asked what I think is the most important principle we teach. Pink and Blue (not wrong, just different) comes to mind, but so does one simple word: goodwill. When you and your spouse see each other as goodwilled, good things are in store for your marriage.

When they first hear the word goodwill, people have questions: Just what is goodwill? How can I know I am showing goodwill toward my spouse? How can I be sure my spouse has goodwill toward me?

A simple definition of goodwill is "the intention to do good toward another person." But the challenge often comes in when one spouse does something to the other spouse that does not feel "good," loving or respectful as the case may be. It is often just a "little thing" but still enough to get *the Crazy Cycle* revving up. At moments like these, the "offendee" has to cut the "offender" some slack, as in giving him or her the "goodwill benefit of the doubt."

A number of verses confirm that goodwill is a biblical idea. See, for example, Proverbs 14:9, Philippians 1:15, and Ephesians 6:7. And Paul is surely talking about the concept of goodwill in 1 Corinthians 7:33–34 when he warns that husbands and wives can become so concerned about pleasing each other that they can be distracted from serving Christ as they should. Granted, husbands and wives don't always demonstrate that natural desire to please each other as well as they might, but their goodwill is real nonetheless.

That's why today's passage is so important. When there is conflict, disagreement, or a bump of some kind, don't automatically conclude that your partner has ill will toward you. If you look for evil (offense), you can find it every time. Do that and *the Crazy Cycle* will spin for sure.

What Proverbs 11:27 is saying to the married couple is this: look for the good in your spouse (even though it seems to be lacking). It is quite likely that you will see your spouse's goodwill coming right back at you. The truth is simple: we will see what we look for. No matter what happens, always assume your partner has basic goodwill toward you. How does that work in real married life? Here are some examples.

I know of one husband who made the decision always to assume his wife had goodwill. Not only did this simple commitment improve his attitude, but it also changed her entire attitude toward him! He writes: "I started giving her the benefit of the doubt . . . I didn't tell her she was disrespectful or anything . . . The results are stunning. She has been easier to live with. She doesn't nag me as much. She has shown increased interest in my hobbies. And she says I am like a new person." All this from simply giving her the benefit of the doubt! What does Proverbs 11:27 say? Look for good and you will find goodwill—sometimes in spades!

Or what about the wife who had to spend much of the summer apart from her husband because of their different career responsibilities? After several weeks she went to see him, meeting him at his office, where she knew he was under a lot of stress because of an important interview coming up. She hoped for at least a hug or a kiss but was greeted instead by a preoccupied husband who practically ignored her. Although she was hurt, she asked God to help her remember he was a goodwilled man who simply needed some time to prepare for an important interview.

Her prayers and patience paid off. Two hours later he "emerged a refreshed and lighter man, full of hugs and kisses for me." They had a wonderful time the rest of the evening, as well as over the next several days. Before learning about goodwill and the Pink and Blue differences between men and women, she would have belittled her preoccupied husband in no uncertain terms. This time she turned to God for understanding and felt true peace because she was able to look at the situation from his male (Blue) point of view.

Does seeking good in your spouse when he or she has not shown much goodwill always work? No, not always, but remember this simple but powerful principle: assuming goodwill in your partner is always the best policy. Keep on seeking the good; eventually you will find it and goodwill as well.

Prayer: Thank the Lord for the goodwill each of you has toward the other. Ask Him for strength to give each other the benefit of the doubt during moments when someone's goodwill seems to be lacking.

Action: During disagreements and conflicts, tell yourself, my spouse has goodwill toward me—even though it doesn't feel that way right now.

For more "husband-friendly devotionals that wives truly love," see Emerson's book The Love & Respect Experience (Thomas Nelson, 2011).

SESSION THREE

In-Session Guide

The Energizing Cycle—C.O.U.P.L.E. Part 1

We have been looking at *the Crazy Cycle*: Without love, she reacts without respect. Without respect, he reacts without love.

Now we wish to consider *the Energizing Cycle*: His _____ motivates her _____. Her _____ motivates his _____.

The question is raised: Who moves first? The one who sees himself or herself as the most mature moves first!

"But Emerson I feel out of control. They cause me to be crazy!" What happens when the phone rings while in an argument with a spouse? True or false: we thought we were out of control but we calmly answered, "Hello."

Put it this way. What if a film crew followed you for six weeks to film you in order to see if you ever got angry at your spouse? What if the reward for not getting angry was $20 million tax free. Would you get angry? No. So, the moral of the story is simple: we just aren't getting paid enough to do the loving and respectful thing!

We have to decide, "Do I have it within me to motivate?" Far more than you can imagine! God would not call you to love and respect but render you impotent in doing this. There is no absolute promise a spouse will respond, but they respond far more than we can imagine. We would respond to them if they acted on this!

Here Is a Principle:

*   We can't motivate a spouse to meet our need for love and respect by refusing to meet their need for love and respect.

We need to be reminded and encouraged: it is never natural to love someone who fails to show respect or respect someone who fails to be loving. This is counter-intuitive. However, this is

_____

_____

_____

_____

_____

_____

_____

_____

_____

normal and there is nothing wrong with us. We are not a fool for obeying Ephesians 5:33. God's command is there because we do not always do this naturally.

So… husbands, here's the overview for you on loving your wife. This will motivate her to respect you! You can do this because you are an honorable man who loves and trusts God's Word! You won't do this perfectly and it will not always feel natural, but you will be amazed at what happens as you act on these six truths!

What Is a Husband's Love?

How to See Through Pink Sunglasses – Loving Her for Who She Is in God's Image!

- When You Want to Be with Her _____ to _____
- When You Aren't Secretly _____ at Her
- When You _____ with Her
- When You _____/_____ with Her
- When You Are Completely _____ to Her
- When You _____ Her above All Else

Will any husband do this perfectly? No! Read Proverbs 24:16!

Emerson prayed, "Why is there not more in the Bible for the pre-married?" The Lord spoke to his heart, "My truth for the married is the game plan I want the pre-married to know."

When a husband loves his wife this way, it keeps them off *The Crazy Cycle*.

C_____ When You Want to Be with Her _____ to _____

Genesis 2:24 For this cause a man shall leave his father and his mother, and shall **cleave** to his wife; and they shall become one flesh.

Genesis 29:34 … my husband will become **attached** to me …

Genesis 30:20 … my husband will **dwell with** me …

_____
_____
_____
_____
_____
_____
_____
_____
_____

Deuteronomy 24:5 When a man takes a new wife, he shall not go out with the army, nor be charged with any duty; **he shall be free at home one year** and shall give happiness to his wife whom he has taken.

Song of Solomon 3:4 ... When I found him whom my soul loves; I **held on to him and would not let him go** ...

Song of Solomon 2:6; 8:3 Let his left hand be under my head and his right hand **embrace** me.

Proverbs 7:11 She is boisterous and rebellious; Her feet do not remain at home ...

When it comes to closeness, the physical act of sex demonstrates to a wife that we desire to be one with her emotionally and spiritually. When we connect sexually, she needs to know this symbolizes that we are connected face to face, heart to heart, and spirit to spirit.

Women give the report face to face to build rapport heart to heart.

Decoding Is Important

Decoding is so important. When a wife reacts in a way that feels disrespectful, a husband should ask himself: Did I just come across in a way that felt unloving to her? Did I send a message to her that I do not want to be close to her face to face and heart to heart?

When it comes to openness, Emerson meditated on Colossians 3:19, asking, "Lord, why should a man love his wife who's making him embittered?" As he reflected, he felt the Lord say to him, "Whatever it is that he thinks she's doing to make him mad, she's not. She's doing what she's doing to be sure that he loves her." And so Paul goes right to the heart: "Just love her. That's the need. She's not trying to make you mad."

Discussion Questions

For Better, Not Worse: A One-Sentence Success Story

Testimony Time: Several of you state briefly what you applied from the last session.

For example . . .

- I chose to trust my spouse's goodwill instead of judging their motives as bad, which I have unthinkingly done before.
- I realized that God has designed some marital conflict to happen so I relaxed more than usual when some tension arose.
- Instead of immediately engaging in *the Crazy Cycle* as I would normally, I tried communicating with my spouse that something they had just done or said had come across as unloving or disrespectful.

1. The Reason for the Command*

In your opinion, why would God command a husband to love his wife even when she appears disrespectful? And why would God command a wife to respect her husband even when he appears unloving?

Discuss how *the Crazy Cycle* can be stopped when a husband and wife obey God's command in Ephesians 5:33.

How is the protective wisdom of God revealed in His commands?

2. Who Moves First?*

If each obstinately refuses to budge until the other changes (she says, "I will be disrespectful until he becomes loving!" or he says, "I will be unloving until she becomes respectful!"), the craziness will continue in this marriage.

How effective is this in motivating the other to love and respect?

The one who sees himself or herself as the most mature moves first.

Every wife knows that if a husband is positive and loving in tone and facial expression, it will touch her heart. Therefore, as a wife, in the quietness of your heart will you commit to move first

_____

_____

_____

_____

_____

_____

_____

_____

and meet your husband's need to feel respected, trusting God for the outcome?

Every husband knows that if a wife is positive and respectful in tone and facial expression, it will touch his heart. Therefore, as a husband, in the quietness of your heart will you commit to move first and meet your wife's need to feel loved, trusting God for the outcome?

3. Motivation

Discuss your thoughts on this idea: "The key to motivating another person is meeting their deepest need."

Does **The Energizing Cycle** make sense to you?

HIS LOVE MOTIVATES HER RESPECT
HER RESPECT MOTIVATES HIS LOVE

In your opinion, why is a wife energized by love to be respectful, and a husband by respect to be loving?

4. What Spells Love to a Wife?

Love to a wife is spelled Closeness, Openness, Understanding, Peacemaking, Loyalty and Esteem (C.O.U.P.L.E.). Briefly state how this acronym is helpful to you as a husband in knowing why your wife might react negatively (*the Crazy Cycle*) and also in assisting you in knowing how to love her better (*the Energizing Cycle*).

CLOSENESS: A Wife Feels Loved When a Husband Is Close Face-to-Face.
5. What Is Going On in This Story?*

[NOTE: As we go into more detail concerning the principles behind C.O.U.P.L.E. and C.H.A.I.R.S. in sessions 3–6, there will be situations with the imperfect but goodwilled couple Stu and Missy to discuss among the group. Though they are fictional, their situations are not. As you discuss, please answer the questions concerning their various activities and conversations honestly among yourselves.]

Missy asks, "Can we be together tonight to talk?" Stu reacts, "What's with you? We just went out a

_____

_____

_____

_____

_____

_____

_____

_____

couple nights ago to that Disney movie. We had dinner with the Smiths at the country club. And last week, we went to the zoo with the kids. You are never satisfied. What do you want? Are we to be Siamese twins? Give me a break."

- What does Missy need?
- Does Stu decode this?
- As a wife, in the past what would your response have been to Stu?
- As a husband, in the past what would your response have been to Missy?
- How does this lead to *the Crazy Cycle*?

6. Cleaving

In Genesis 2:24 we learn that a husband is to cleave to his wife. What do you think "to cleave" means?

1. Sexual intimacy
2. Face-to-face talking
3. Heart-to-heart closeness
4. All of the above

7. The Nature of a Woman

Already at age four my daughter Joy was saying, "Daddy, look at me!" whenever she wanted to talk. She wanted to talk eye-to-eye. At that age she had already concluded that if I was not looking, I was not listening. She would grab my cheeks and turn my face toward her.

As well, around the world women gather to talk. Go into any cappuccino café and you'll see two or three women seated at a round table talking face-to-face expressing their concerns and wishes for at least an hour.

Men, reflect on your own marriage. How does your wife express her need to spend time with you alone, face-to-face? How have you seen this result in her feeling loved?

8. The Nature of a Man

Men tend to look away during times of conflict and provocation, seeking to prevent things from escalating out of control. Why do some couples fail to see this as an honorable approach?

_____

_____

_____

_____

_____

_____

_____

_____

_____

As a wife, when your husband looks away, can you accept that? Discuss how this realization would affect your response during *the Crazy Cycle*.

On the other hand, even though it is natural for a man to look away and get away to calm things down, how does this often feel unloving to his wife?

A mature man of honor will move first and meet his wife's need for closeness even though he prefers moving away from her during heated exchanges. Discuss the ramifications of this action for a couple caught in *the Crazy Cycle*.

Immediate Application

Write down in the space below one or two things that came to mind during this session that you already know you need to begin applying or practicing this week.

Midweek Devotional

Who Makes the First Move in Your Marriage?

Solid food is for those who are mature, who through training have the skill to recognize the difference between right and wrong.

—Hebrews 5:14 NLT

People always ask, "Who moves first to get off *the Crazy Cycle* and onto *the Energizing Cycle?*" I always reply, "I prayed about the answer, and I heard the Lord's inaudible voice: the one who sees himself or herself as the most mature moves first."

Early on, when I shared that an ttswer, I wondered if people would resist the idea because it suggests somebody always has to make the first move, and this doesn't sound "fair." Most of us want the other person to move first at least half the time. After many years, however, I have the confidence to say that this comment positively motivates most people. Why? Because most spouses see themselves as mature and able "to recognize the difference between right and wrong" (Hebrews 5:14).

A husband writes: "Who moves first? If it is the one who is the most mature (and I believe that I am mature), I have no excuse. It doesn't matter who hurt first. I've shared that insight with a lot of people because of the difference it made in my conduct."

Another man says: "We have two young daughters, aged four and seven. I want to be the mature one who breaks the cycle and turns things around. I know that this is what God wills and what is best for my family. It is difficult and I am not perfect, but I am working to show my wife unconditional love."

A wife e-mails: "I made a decision at that moment that my life was going to count for something for the kingdom. To me, that meant learning my Bible and obeying God in my marriage and every part of my life. I am the mature one and I needed to go first. That always made me mad before, and now I am accepting that God requires it of me. God got hold of my heart that day in a way as never before."

As these letters attest, mature moves by goodwilled spouses positively influence the marriage in God's direction. But what does moving first look like? Maturity manifests itself in multiple ways. Some examples:

During a moment of "heated fellowship," Steven softens his raised voice in response to Tanya's even louder voice. She clearly hears his olive branch.

After Susan spouts off disrespectful words on the heels of Richard's unloving comments, she apologizes first, saying, "I am sorry for my disrespect."

Gary makes a to-do list of undone tasks around the house that are driving Lisa nuts. He takes an entire Saturday to take care of them, even though Lisa won't listen to his pleas to be more disciplined about the budget.

Even though Tom fails to spend as much time with Lindsay as she wishes, she resolves to stop her tardiness so he doesn't have to wait for her in the car.

Is moving first always fair? No, of course not. There are times when it seems crystal clear which one should move first. But this isn't about "justice" or what is fair. It's about sucking it up and biting the bullet to stop the insanity of *the Crazy Cycle* and enjoy the motivation of *the Energizing Cycle*. As Hebrews 5 says, spiritual milk is for babies and solid food is for the mature ones who can recognize the right thing and then just do it.

First move, anyone?

Prayer: Thank the Lord for setting the example of always making the first move. Ask Him for the wisdom and strength to make the first move for each other in every situation, minor or major. Ask Him to help you stop *The Crazy Cycle* and stay on *The Energizing Cycle*, motivated by love and respect

Action: This coming week (or month), practice being the mature one who makes the first move. Talk together about how it feels when one of you makes the first move to end a stalemate—and *The Crazy Cycle*.

For more "husband-friendly devotionals that wives truly love," see Emerson's book The Love & Respect Experience *(Thomas Nelson, 2011).*

SESSION FOUR

In-Session Guide
The Energizing Cycle—C.O.U.P.L.E. Part 2

O_____ When You Aren't Secretly _____ at Her

Colossians 3:19 Husbands, love your wives, and do **not be embittered** against them.

Malachi 2:14-15 ... the Lord has been a witness between you and the wife of your youth, against whom you have dealt treacherously, though she is your companion and your wife by covenant ... **Take heed then, to your spirit,** and let no one deal treacherously against the wife of your youth.

Judges 19:3 ... her husband ... went after her to **speak tenderly** to her ...

Judges 14:7 So he went down and **talked** to the woman; and she looked good to Samson.

Proverbs 21:19 It is better to live in a desert land, than with a ... vexing woman.

Deuteronomy 28:56 The refined and delicate woman ... who would not venture to set the sole of her foot on the ground for delicateness and refinement, shall be hostile toward the husband she cherishes.

U_____ When You _____ With Her

1 Peter 3:7 You husbands likewise, live with [your wives] **in an understanding way,** as with a weaker vessel, since she is a woman ... so that your prayers may not be hindered.

1 Samuel 1:8 Then Elkanah her husband said to her, "Hannah, **why** do you weep and **why** do you not eat and **why** is your heart sad? Am I not better to you than ten sons?"

1 Samuel 25:3 Nabal, and his wife's name was Abigail ... the man was **harsh and evil** in his dealings.

Job 2:8-9 And he took a potsherd to scrape himself while he was sitting among the ashes. Then his wife said to him, "Do you still hold fast your integrity? Curse God and die!"

_____

_____

_____

_____

_____

_____

_____

_____

_____

P_____ When You _____/_____ With Her

1 Corinthians 7:28 But if you marry, you have not sinned … Yet such **will have trouble in this life** …

Matthew 19:5-6 For this cause a man shall leave his father and mother, and shall cleave to his wife; and the two shall **become one** flesh. Consequently, they are **no longer two**, but one flesh. What therefore God has joined **together**, let no man **separate.**

Mark 3:25 If a **house is divided** against itself, that house will not be able to stand.

Ephesians 5:21-22 … be **subject to one another** in the fear of Christ... wives ... husbands ...

Isaiah 54:6 Like a wife **forsaken** and **grieved** in spirit, even like a wife of one's youth when she is **rejected**.

1 Corinthians 7:3-4 The wife does not have authority over her own body, but the husband does; and likewise also **the husband does not have authority** over his own body, but the wife does.

Genesis 3:12 "The **woman** whom **You** gave to be with me, she gave me from the tree, and I ate."

Proverbs 30:20 … She eats and wipes her mouth, and says, "I have done no wrong."

1 Corinthians 7:11 If she does leave, let her remain unmarried, or else be reconciled to her husband.

L_____ When You Are Completely_____ to Her

Malachi 2:14 ... the wife of your youth ... she is your companion and your wife by **covenant**.

Malachi 2:16 "**For I hate divorce,**" says the Lord. So take heed to your spirit, that you do not deal treacherously.

Hebrews 13:4 Let marriage be **held in honor** among all, and let the marriage bed be undefiled; for fornicators and adulterers God will judge.

Job 31:1 I have made a **covenant** with my eyes; how then could I gaze at a virgin?

Proverbs 2:17 … that leaves the companion of her youth, and forgets the covenant of her God.

_____
_____
_____
_____
_____
_____
_____
_____
_____

E_____ When You _____ Her Above All Else

1 Peter 3:7 You husbands … as with a weaker vessel since she is a woman; and **grant her honor as a fellow heir** of the grace of life, so that your prayers may not be hindered.

Ephesians 5:29 For no one ever hated his own flesh, but nourishes and **cherishes** it, just as Christ also [does] the church …

Proverbs 31:28 … her husband … he **praises** her …

Song of Solomon 7:6 … how **delightful** you are, My love …

2 Samuel 6:16-22 … Michal … saw … David … dancing before the Lord; and she despised him in her heart … David said… "I will be more lightly esteemed …"

_____

_____

_____

_____

_____

_____

_____

_____

_____

_____

_____

_____

_____

_____

_____

_____

_____

_____

_____

_____

_____

_____

_____

_____

_____

_____

Discussion Questions

For Better, Not Worse: A One-Sentence Success Story

Testimony Time: Several of you state briefly what you applied from the last session.

> For example . . .

- When my wife talked to me I looked at her eye-to-eye and face-to-face instead of looking away.
- I attempted to move first.
- I noticed the differences in my spouse's nature when it comes to closeness, and said to myself, "Not wrong, just different."

OPENNESS: A Wife Feels an Openness When You Aren't Secretly Mad at Her

1. What Is Going On in This Story?*

Feeling frustrated and angry over losing eight thousand dollars on an investment, Stu says in response to Missy's request to talk, "Look, I'm tired. I do not want to talk right now, okay?" He turns on the news. She tries again later to bring some things up about his day but he only says, "I don't want to talk about it. Can't we just have some peace and quiet around here?"

She then inquires, "Well, when can we talk?" He angrily retorts, "I don't know."

- What does Missy need?
- Does Stu decode this?
- As a wife, in the past what would your response have been to Stu?
- As a husband, in the past what would your response have been to Missy?
- How does this lead to *the Crazy Cycle*?

2. Personalizing Conflict

When it comes to intimate relationships, wives tend to personalize conflict more than husbands do. This explains why she asks, "Can we talk?" She wants to connect in order to be reassured that you're not mad at her. On the other hand, men feel interrogated by "Can we talk?"

Does this echo your experience as a couple? Explain.

_____

_____

_____

_____

_____

_____

_____

_____

_____

3. Truthful Yet Loving

As a man of honor, what have you learned about being more open with your wife?

What should Stu have said to Missy to set her heart at rest?

What if Stu had been mad at Missy about something—how can a husband be open without crushing his wife's spirit?

Wives, share with the group how men can speak the truth in love without crushing your spirit.

4. Sexuality

Though a husband may not be as open as his wife hopes, he can be more open than he has been. And, as he opens emotionally, she tends to open sexually. Does this make sense? Why or why not?

UNDERSTANDING: A Wife Feels Loved When a Husband Understands Her
5. What Is Going On in This Story?*

Missy complains to Stu, "The kids refused to go to bed the night you left for Kansas City. The phone rang at 11:30 p.m., which was a prank call and frightened me, and then the next day the electricity went out in the snow storm. On top of all that, I put on four pounds from Christmas parties and I have nothing to wear."

Stu, reading the Tribune says, "Do you have to talk about this now? I'm trying to read the stock market listings. You are always interfering with my time. Besides I've told you countless times before that things are never as bad as you imagine. You get yourself worked up way too much. You need to do what I do. Let some of these things roll off you like water off a duck's back."

- What does Missy need?
- Does Stu decode this?
- As a wife, in the past what would your response have been to Stu?
- As a husband, in the past what would your response have been to Missy?
- How does this lead to *the Crazy Cycle*?

_____

_____

_____

_____

_____

_____

_____

_____

_____

_____

6. An Understanding Way

In 1 Peter 3:7 Peter wrote, "You husbands in the same way, live with your wives in an understanding way . . . since she is a woman."

In your opinion, what would it mean for Stu to live with Missy in a more understanding way?

7. Solution Versus Listening Ear

Emerson shares that they experienced a new energy in their marriage when he learned to ask Sarah, "Do you need a listening ear, or do you need a solution to the problem?" Explain the difference between the two and why sometimes getting to a solution is not what is needed at the time.

8. Teapot

Like a teapot that boils and then whistles to release the steam, a wife can experience an emotional overload and need to ventilate to someone who empathizes.

Women, do you agree that talking about your problems and receiving assurance that you are understood brings you relief even though there's no solution? Explain.

Since the husband is the Christ figure and the wife is the church figure according to Ephesians 5, it is natural for her to want to place her burdens upon her husband in the same way the church places its burdens upon Christ. What are your thoughts on this?

9. Emotional Release Versus Sexual Release

A husband says, "Well, I know she needs emotional release, but it is the same thing over and over again." Similarly—without being crass—most husbands need sexual release and it is the same thing over and over again!

Many times we are critical of our spouse because we do not have the same need that they have and consequently we view their need as excessive or marginal. But when we look more deeply we realize we have a comparable need—though different—which is equally as intense. What are your thoughts when Emerson says, "Not wrong, just different," related to this issue?

_____
_____
_____
_____
_____
_____
_____
_____

PEACEMAKING: A Wife Feels at Peace When Issues are Resolved
10. What Is Going On in This Story?*

Missy drove the restored '57 Chevy to the grocery store because Stu took the van to work. While driving through puddles, mud splashed all over it. When Stu saw it, he was mad. He had recently waxed it. Missy kept saying, "I'm sorry," but Stu ignored her and went to the garage. She came out to say again she was sorry, but he gave her the cold shoulder. He didn't talk to her until later that night when she again approached him. But all he said was, "Just drop it!" Several days later another argument arose on some other topic, and she brought up the '57 Chevy, that he hadn't forgiven her, and didn't love her.

- He reacted, "What's the car have to do with this? You just look for things to criticize me for." Missy walks off crying.
- What does Missy need?
- Does Stu decode this?
- As a wife, in the past what would your response have been to Stu?
- As a husband, in the past what would your response have been to Missy?
- How does this lead to *the Crazy Cycle*?

11. Trouble

This bears repeating from Session 1. The apostle Paul says in 1 Corinthians 7:28 that if two people marry they have not sinned but they will have trouble. For example, in 1 Corinthians 7:4 we read that the wife does not have authority over her own body but the husband does, and the husband does not have authority over his own body but the wife does.

In this instance, each has equal authority in the sexual realm. Therefore, who decides if they are going to be sexually intimate tonight?

From this verse, we clearly learn that some conflict is designed by God. Therefore God expects couples to learn to resolve things in a peacemaking way.

How does this knowledge that God orchestrates some conflict in marriage, give you a greater confidence that He will help you resolve issues?

12. She Gets Historical

We make the point that it can be the honorable thing for a husband to say, "Let's just drop this argument and move on." How does this feel unloving to a wife?

Most women, though not all, have a tendency to want to talk things through more fully. This includes a need to talk about how each was feeling, and to make sure that there are mutual apologies. With this in mind, explain what is going on when a husband says "drop it" and his wife gets "historical," resurfacing past issues from other arguments.

LOYALTY: A Wife Feels Loyalty When You Are Completely Committed to Her

13. What Is Going On in This Story?*

Missy asks Stu, "Will you always be with me? Will you still want me when I am old and gray? What if I become an invalid or lose my mind?"

Stu comments, "Hey, I told you I loved you the day we married. If anything changes, I'll tell you. What's the matter, scared I'll trade you in for a new model? Just keep yourself looking good and I'll keep you around."

- What does Missy need?
- Does Stu decode this?
- As a wife, in the past what would your response have been to Stu?
- As a husband, in the past what would your response have been to Missy?
- How does this lead to *the Crazy Cycle*?

14. The Covenant

Malachi 2:14 says about one's wife, "she is your companion and your wife by covenant." Would several men in the group share what it means to them that they have made a covenant with God and their wives?

15. A Husband's Commitment

In Dr. James Dobson's February 2001 newsletter, he shared this story: "My friends Keith and Mary Korstjens have been married for more than forty years. Shortly after their honeymoon, Mary

_____

_____

_____

_____

_____

_____

_____

_____

_____

_____

was stricken with polio and became a quadriplegic. The doctors informed her that she would be confined to a wheelchair for the rest of her life. It was a devastating development, but Keith never wavered in his commitment to Mary. For all these years he has bathed and dressed her, carried her to and from her bed, taken her to the bathroom, brushed her teeth, and combed her hair. Obviously, Keith could have divorced Mary in 1957 and looked for a new, healthier wife, but he never even considered it. I admire this man, not only for doing the right thing, but for continuing to love and cherish his wife. Though the problems you and I face may be less challenging than those encountered by the Korstjens family, all of us will have our own difficulties. How will we respond? Some will give up on marriage for some pretty flimsy reasons. If we are going to go the distance, nothing short of an ironclad commitment will sustain us when the hard times come."

What do you think it takes to make the kind of commitment Keith made to Mary?

In acknowledging that we will all face challenges in marriage, Dr. Dobson states the following: "How will we respond? Some will give up on marriage for some pretty flimsy reasons." Share your thoughts on the importance of decoding unloving and disrespectful attitudes to avoid divorcing for "flimsy reasons."

16. God Hates Divorce

What does Malachi 2:16 mean to you? "'For I hate divorce,' says the Lord, the God of Israel . . .'"

ESTEEM: A Wife Feels Esteemed When You Treasure Her Above All Else

17. What Is Going On in This Story?*

Feeling like a failure as a mother, Missy was depressed. With tears in her eyes she says to Stu, "Mothering is everything to me, but I feel like I am flunking. Am I doing anything right?" Stu replies, "Well, I can see what you are saying. Maybe you need to get together with some older mothers for help."

- What does Missy need?
- Does Stu decode this?
- As a wife, in the past what would your response have been to Stu?
- As a husband, in the past what would your response have been to Missy?
- How does this lead to *the Crazy Cycle*?

_____

_____

_____

_____

_____

_____

_____

_____

_____

18. Honor Her as an Equal

What does the following verse mean to you? "You husbands . . . show her honor as a fellow heir of the grace of life" (1 Peter 3:7).

Because a wife has equal worth in the eyes of God, she is to be treated with esteem.

Though a wife fails, as a husband fails, how can a husband build his wife up?

Though she is inadequate as he is weak in many areas, how can he express appreciation for all she does and let her know he treasures the person she is to him? Give specific examples.

19. She Has a Different Point System

What seems to be an insignificant action by the husband, like buying a diet book, can put him a million points in the red. On the other side, writing a little love note, letting her know that he prizes her for the many sacrifices she makes as a mother, which the kids do not acknowledge, can be three million points in the black!

Do you agree or disagree that women have a different point system when it comes to feeling esteemed?

Immediate Application

Write down in the space below one or two things that came to mind during this session that you already know you need to begin applying or practicing this week.

_____

_____

_____

_____

_____

_____

_____

_____

_____

_____

_____

_____

_____

_____

_____

_____

_____

Midweek Devotional

Sex and Affection: A Two-Way Street

The husband should fulfill his marital duty to his wife,
and likewise the wife to her husband.

—1 Corinthians 7:3 NIV

Feeling that his sexual appetites are waning, the husband asks his doctor if something might be wrong. The doc says, "Walk five miles a day for the next three weeks and call me and tell me how you're doing." Three weeks later the husband calls, and the doc asks, "So . . . how is the sex?" The husband replies, "How am I supposed to know? I haven't seen my wife in three weeks, and I'm 105 miles from home."

"So . . . how is the sex?" If there was ever an issue that can quickly become a love and respect issue, it is this. Fortunately, Paul leaves some good advice to help couples keep sex in a positive perspective, providing they are willing to work together to benefit one another. He says, "The husband should fulfill his marital duty to his wife, and likewise the wife to her husband" (1 Corinthians 7:3). That's what it says in the New International Version, and almost the same wording is in the New American Standard Bible. At first glance it sounds as though Paul thinks sex is an obligation, to be done begrudgingly if necessary. And, true enough, the Greek word here for "duty" means we are to give the other person what is due, as if we have a debt to pay.

There is, however, another way to translate this Greek word that throws light on the problem: "Husbands and wives should be fair with each other about having sex" (CEV). And in the Phillips translation we read: "The husband should give to his wife what is due to her as his wife, and the wife should be as fair to her husband." When fair play precedes foreplay, husband and wife are tuned in on satisfying each other sexually and affectionately: "Let the husband render to his wife the affection due her, and likewise also the wife to her husband" (NKJV). Each is focusing on giving, not receiving, and that makes sex an entirely different ball game from the one too many couples play, which often leads to making it an issue that obscures the Real Issue: feeling unloved or disrespected.

Over the years I have received literally thousands of emails from spouses who struggle with the issue of being fair with each other about sex. Typically, the husband's primary need is for sexual release, which only his wife can meet, and the wife's primary need is for affection and a feeling of emotional connectedness. (There are exceptions to these general leanings. For example, I get e-mails from a substantial number of women who say they are the ones who need sex more often.)

Not surprisingly, if one spouse's need is not met, he or she will not be inclined to want to focus on the need of the other. And so it seems to be a standoff. The wife can say, "Lovingly meet my needs for affection and connection and I'll respond sexually." The husband can answer, "Respectfully meet my sexual need, since you alone can meet that need, and I'll respond to your emotional needs." This is the kind of quid pro quo dance many couples do, but it is not what Paul means in 1 Corinthians 7 when he talks about being fair to one another. Obviously, Paul is not saying one spouse can mandate "sex for affection" or that the other can mandate "affection for sex."

Sex and affection are the best proving grounds to help you and your spouse grow in love and respect for each other—physically, emotionally, and intimately. Look at the sexual aspect of your relationship as a compliment to how important you are in your spouse's life. You are the only person who can meet this need in your spouse!

If one partner is not being as responsive as the other might like, Christ is calling someone to make the first move. (Maybe He is calling both of you!) As two mature people, can you talk it through and work it out? There is no need to go three weeks without sex or affection and wind up "105 miles from home."

Prayer: Thank God that you both have needs only the other can meet. Pray for the wisdom to meet those needs fairly with mutual concern for one another.

Action: Having devotions about sex can draw you closer or possibly start up *the Crazy Cycle*. Share honestly with each other about your needs on this two-way street. Talk together or possibly write each other notes about your needs as lovingly and respectfully as you can. If sex continues to be a serious issue, consider seeing a skilled Christian counselor.

For more "husband-friendly devotionals that wives truly love," see Emerson's book The Love & Respect Experience (Thomas Nelson, 2011).

In-Session Guide

The Energizing Cycle—C.H.A.I.R.S. Part 1

What Is a Wife's Respect?

The Crazy Cycle says:

> *WITHOUT LOVE SHE REACTS WITHOUT RESPECT*
> *WITHOUT RESPECT HE REACTS WITHOUT LOVE*

Few wives mean to be disrespectful. They say, "He should know that I don't mean it!" Even so, the reaction feels disrespectful to a husband and he tends to react by stonewalling and withdrawing, which feels unloving to a wife. Thus, they spin on *the Crazy Cycle*!

Few men are narcissistic, but instead they simply have a need to feel respected for who they are as human beings created in God's image. It raises the question: How does a wife put on respect without respecting unrespectable behavior?! The answer is simple: she respectfully confronts what feels unloving to her.

But beyond that she can be proactive. She can actually meet a need in her husband for respect. However, this seems counter-intuitive to her. It doesn't feel natural. Even the idea of making respect a priority doesn't seem right. She believes as a woman that her love should motivate his love and his love motivate her love and they will all be happy! She prefers to love him the way she needs love. But God made us male and female. Not wrong, just different. God reveals truth to every wife into the masculine soul. This session helps her understand how God made the husband male and that when she meets the following needs she motivates her man to love!

Not all buy into this! Here is what some wives have said to me.

"Emerson, I'm not feeling respect for him, and I refuse to be a hypocrite who does something she doesn't feel. You show respect to your superiors. He's not superior to me. I'm not inferior to him. Also, respect must be earned, and he hasn't earned it. He doesn't deserve it. Furthermore, I'm not going to give him license to do what he wants. I'm not going to feed his narcissism. I'm certainly not going to return to patriarchal times and fear male dominance. I'm not going to lose a sense of my identity. And, I'm not going to subject myself to emotional abuse. But other than these things, Dr. Emerson, I'm really open to hear what you have to say about this."

_____

_____

_____

_____

_____

_____

_____

_____

These feelings are real, but every wife must trust in God's wisdom and goodness in revealing this truth to her in Ephesians 5:33 and 1 Peter 3:1-2.

Remember the Respect Test: "I was thinking of you today and all the things about you that I respect, and I want you to know that I respect you." Say it and leave the room and watch what happens!

Communication is not the key to a marriage. Mutual understanding is. If she only speaks Spanish and he only speaks German, there will not be mutual understanding and thus neither will communicate well! A husband speaks the Respect language and a wife speaks the Love language. Both must learn the other's vocabulary in order to communicate. The below information is the mother-tongue of every male.

How to See Through Blue Sunglasses - Respect Him for Who He Is in God's Image!

- Appreciating His Desire to _____ and _____ (emphasis is on desire not performance)
- Appreciating His Desire to _____ and _____ (and even die)
- Appreciating His Desire to Be _____ and to _____ (make _____)
- Appreciating His Desire to _____ and _____
- Appreciating His Desire for a Shoulder-to-Shoulder _____
- Appreciating His Desire for _____ Intimacy

C_____ Appreciating His Desire to _____ and _____

Genesis 2:15 The Lord God took the man and put him into the **garden** of Eden to **cultivate and keep it.**

Genesis 2:18 God said, "It is not good for the man to be alone; I will make him a **helper suitable** for him."

Genesis 3:19 By the sweat of your face You shall eat bread, till you return to the **ground** ...

1 Corinthians 11:9 For indeed man was not created for the woman's sake, but woman **for the man's sake.**

Titus 2:5 Workers at home ...

_____

_____

_____

_____

_____

_____

_____

_____

_____

Discussion Questions

For Better, Not Worse: A One-Sentence Success Story

Testimony Time: Several of you state briefly what you applied from the last session.

For example . . .

- I found that when he is more open emotionally, it makes our relationship more romantic.
- When I spoke more openly and truthfully, I also tried to say it more lovingly as a man of honor.
- I held my tongue when tempted to put my wife down. I realized anew this is unnecessary, dishonors her, and makes her feel inferior.

1. Motivation

We said earlier, "The key to motivating another person is meeting their deepest need." What is your understanding of this idea?

Does **the Energizing Cycle** make sense to you?

HIS LOVE MOTIVATES HER RESPECT

HER RESPECT MOTIVATES HIS LOVE

CONQUEST: Respecting His Desire to Work and Achieve

2. What Is Going On in This Story?*

Missy says to Stu, "I am sick and tired of you choosing work over the family. You get up early and come home late. You don't care about me or the kids. Yes, I got your message about your promotion, but I don't care. This is all about you. You have fun all day long, and give me very little of yourself. When you are home, you fall asleep watching TV. We never talk. Well, I am thinking about going back to school and I need to talk to you about this tonight. You are going to need to financially support me in this. Right now, though, you need to pick up the kids again from their lessons. And, you need to take the check over to Molly Maids; I forgot to pay them for cleaning the house. I stayed too long at the athletic club today talking to my friends."

_____

_____

_____

_____

_____

_____

_____

_____

_____

- What does Stu need?
- Does Missy decode this?
- As a husband, in the past what would your response have been to Missy?
- How does this lead to *the Crazy Cycle*?

3. Call Versus Freedom of Choice

A husband feels called to work outside the home. On the other hand, a wife views her own work outside the home as a freedom-of-choice issue—an option, not an obligation. She wants the freedom to have babies and freedom to take care of them full-time. If she decides to be a full-time mommy, she expects her husband to care for her and the family. If she wants a career, that is her choice for herself.

Do you agree or disagree? Explain.

4. What Do You Do?

Genesis 2:15 says, "The Lord God took the man and put him into the garden of Eden to cultivate it and keep it." In Paradise, Adam was created to work!

What is the first question every man asks another man when meeting for the first time?

Agree or disagree?

1. There is something deep in the soul of a male that finds his personal identity in what he does.

2. A woman finds her identity related to her family (she is her son's mother, to quote one famous female radio broadcaster).

5. The Helper Suitable

In Genesis 2:18 God says, "It is not good for the man to be alone; I will make him a helper suitable for him." What does this say about God's design for women?

When first dating your husband, did you admire him and his dreams and cheer him on about his longings to make a difference in his world? Did you come across as one who wanted to help him in these pursuits? As couples, reflect on whether this has changed in your relationship and why.

_____

_____

_____

_____

_____

_____

_____

_____

_____

6. Meal Ticket

Times have changed. Many women are working full-time outside the home, bringing in as much money as their husbands. Yet many men still express a sense that they are viewed by their wives as nothing more than a meal ticket, feeling second to the children in her eyes, and unappreciated for his contributions.

Men, can you shed some light on these thoughts?

7. Decoding

Wives, when your husband is reacting unloving, sometimes sulking and being moody, could it be that he feels little respect for the long hours he puts in at work? Share your thoughts.

Immediate Application

Write down in the space below one or two things that came to mind during this session that you already know you need to begin applying or practicing this week.

Midweek Devotional

If Only We Didn't Have Money Problems

*And my God will supply all your needs according to
His riches in glory in Christ Jesus.*

—Philippians 4:19

"Emerson, we agree with the Love & Respect message, but we have money problems. We'd have a really great marriage if we didn't have these financial pressures."

I receive many e-mails just like this, from couples who believe lack of money is the root of their marital problems. I understand why they say that. Financial problems can cause tremendous pressures and frustrations. In fact, many marriage experts claim that money mismanagement is the main source of marital discord. Yes, money problems are very real, but they are not the root reason that friendship and intimacy fade as she feels unloved and he feels disrespected. Money squabbles don't undermine love and respect; they simply reveal unloving and disrespectful attitudes, which are the real reason why a marriage can start to wobble on *the Crazy Cycle*.

During a heated discussion about money, it is all too easy to appear hostile, sarcastic, or even contemptuous. It may be for only a few seconds, but it is enough to deflate the spirit of your spouse. Mark it down: money problems simply reveal what is in our hearts, how mature or immature we really are. Ouch! That hurts, I know, but it can be true of any of us.

Think of a toddler who throws himself kicking on the floor when he realizes he cannot have what he wants at the store. Being deprived of what he wants does not cause his temper tantrums; it simply reveals his immaturity. But what about us when we are deprived of what we want? Does being an adult guarantee that we will not overreact when we find ourselves in a financial situation contrary to our liking?

Some spouses think, if we just had more money, then we'd be happy. How different, really, is this reasoning from that of a little kid, lying there kicking on the floor, thinking, if I can just get Mom to buy me that piece of candy, then I will be happy?

Immaturity on someone's part may or may not be at least part of any couple's money problems. But what exactly do you do when once again there is more month than money and you find tempers are about to flare? All kinds of money problems can suddenly descend. The question is, will a couple confront these problems together, showing each other love and respect, or will they turn away from each other and even the Lord because of anger and frustration?

When money problems close in, we have our best opportunity to deepen our maturity. The struggle to deal with money will remain real, but how glorious to wade through this quagmire as a team and be confident in God to lead us out of the predicament. The choice is always ours. Ultimately, financial needs should cause two people to turn to Christ for His supply, and what a glorious promise in today's key verse! God will supply our needs, but He wants us to be able to tell the difference between our needs and our wants.

Suppose, for example, you need transportation to work, and you have just enough cash to pay for a pre-owned vehicle with decent miles that has been well cared for. But at the last second, you spot a practically new convertible in mint condition. Of course, it costs a lot more, but you manage to finance it and drive off the lot feeling you got what you always wanted. Yes, you did. But in six months the big payments are putting you under severe financial stress. What happened to that promise in Philippians 4:19? It is still there. He nicely provided for your need with that older vehicle, but you wanted that convertible and you wound up with money problems.

King Solomon, who knew quite a bit about making poor decisions, said, "The stupidity of a person turns his life upside down, and his heart rages against the Lord" (Proverbs 19:3 GW). Raging against the Lord for not providing enough for our wants is childish. Instead, we can put James 1:5 into action. Does it say God will drop the money into our laps? No, but it does promise the wisdom to budget carefully and find the Lord providing a way when there seems to be no way. As He parted the Red Sea for Moses, the Lord can part our "seas of red"—if we let Him!

Prayer: Thank the Lord for any money problems you may have at the moment, because they give you the opportunity to trust Him more. Ask Him to supply your needs, as He shows you what to do to meet your financial obligations.

Action: Sort out together your needs and your wants. Be honest with each other, but always with love and respect. If your financial challenges are severe, you may want to consider seeing a skilled Christian counselor.

For more "husband-friendly devotionals that wives truly love," see Emerson's book The Love & Respect Experience (Thomas Nelson, 2011).

In-Session Guide

The Energizing Cycle—C.H.A.I.R.S. Part 2

H_____ Appreciating His Desire to _____ and
_____

Ephesians 5:23-24 For the husband is **the head** of the wife, as Christ also is the head of the church, He Himself [being] the Savior of the body. But **as the church is subject** ["hupotasso"] to Christ, so also the wives [ought to be] to their husbands in everything.

1 Timothy 5:8 But if anyone does not **provide** for his own, and especially for those of his household, he has denied the faith, and is worse than an unbeliever.

Nehemiah 4:14 ... **fight for** your ... wives, and your houses.

Ephesians 5:22; Colossians 3:18; 1 Peter 3:1; 1 Corinthians 11:3; Titus 2:5

  Proverbs 31:24 She makes linen garments and sells them, and supplies belts to the tradesmen.

  Proverbs 31:27 She looks well to the ways of her household, and does not eat the bread of idleness.

A_____ Appreciating His Desire to Be _____ and to
_____

1 Corinthians 16:13 ... act like men, be **strong** ...

1 Kings 2:2 Be strong, therefore, and **show yourself a man.**

1 Timothy 3:5 ... if a man does not know how to **manage his own household** ...

1 Timothy 3:12 ... **good managers** ...

1 Timothy 2:12 But I do not allow a woman to ... **exercise authority** over a man, but to remain **quiet**.

_____
_____
_____
_____
_____
_____
_____
_____
_____

Isaiah 3:12 … **women rule** over them …

Genesis 3:16 … your husband, and he shall **rule** over you.

1 Peter 3:1-2, 4 … disobedient … husbands … may be won without a word by the behavior of their wives, as they observe your … respectful behavior … but [let it be] the hidden person of the heart, with the imperishable quality of **a gentle and quiet spirit,** which is precious in the sight of God.

Proverbs 19:13 … the **contentions** of a wife are a constant dripping.

Judges 14:16f And Samson's wife wept before him … "You only hate me, and you do not love me …" she wept before him seven days … And … he told her because she **pressed him so hard** … And his anger burned.

Judges 16:15-16 She said to him, "How can you say, 'I love you,' when your heart is not with me?" … she pressed him daily with her words and urged him, **that his soul was annoyed to death.**

Proverbs 31:16 She considers a field and buys it; from her earnings she plants a vineyard.

1 Corinthians 12:28 And God has appointed in the church … administrations …

Romans 12:8 He who leads …

I_____ Appreciating His Desire to_____ and

_____

Ephesians 5:25-26 Husbands, **love your wives** … **sanctify her** … **with the word.**

1 Timothy 2:14 … it was not Adam who was **deceived,** but the woman being quite deceived, fell into transgression.

2 Corinthians 11:3 But I am afraid, lest as the serpent **deceived** Eve by his craftiness …

Genesis 3:17 Then to Adam He said, "Because you have **listened to the voice of your wife** …"

Deuteronomy 13:6 If … the wife you cherish … **entice you secretly,** saying, "Let us go and serve other gods …"

Job 2:10 He said to her, "You speak as one of the **foolish women** speaks …"

Proverbs 9:13 The woman of folly is boisterous; she is naive, and **knows nothing.**

_____

_____

_____

_____

_____

_____

_____

_____

Proverbs 12:4 An excellent wife is the crown of her husband ... she who **shames him** is rottenness to his bones.

1 Samuel 1:8 Then Elkanah her husband said to her, "Hannah, **why** do you weep and **why** do you not eat and **why** is your heart sad? Am I not better to you than ten sons?"

Genesis 30:1-2 She said to Jacob, "Give me children, or **else I die.**" Then Jacob's anger burned against Rachel, and he said, "Am I in the place of God ...?"

2 Timothy 3:6 ... captivate weak women weighed down with sins, **led on by various impulses.**

Proverbs 30:20 She eats and wipes her mouth, and says, **"I have done no wrong."**

> **Proverbs 19:14** ... a prudent wife is from the Lord.

> **Proverbs 31:26** She opens her mouth in wisdom.

> **Luke 18:9** And He also told this parable to some people who trusted in themselves that they were righteous, and viewed others with contempt ...

> **Luke 10:40** But Martha ... came up to Him and said, "Lord, do You not care ...?"

R_____ Appreciating His Desire for a Shoulder-to-Shoulder _____

Titus 2:3-4 ... encourage the young women **to love** [phileo] their husbands ...

Song of Solomon 5:1,16 ... friends ... O lovers ... This is my beloved and this is **my friend** ...

Proverbs 31:11-12 ... she **does him good** and not evil all the days of her life.

Proverbs 31:26 ... the teaching of **kindness** is on her tongue.

1 Corinthians 7:11 ... let her ... be **reconciled to her husband.**

Malachi 2:14 ... She is your **companion** and your wife ...

> **Proverbs 7:11** She is boisterous and rebellious; her feet do not remain at home ...

> **Proverbs 2:17** ... That leaves the companion of her youth, and forgets the covenant of her God

> **Proverbs 21:9** It is better to live in a corner of a roof, than in a house shared with a contentious woman.

_____
_____
_____
_____
_____
_____
_____
_____
_____

S _____ Appreciating His Desire for _____ Intimacy

Proverbs 5:19 Let **her breasts satisfy you** at all times; be exhilarated always with her love.

Matthew 5:28 … everyone who looks on a woman to **lust** for her has committed adultery with her … in his heart.

1 Corinthians 7:4-5 The wife does not have authority over her own body, but the husband [does]; and likewise also the husband does not have authority over his own body, but the wife [does]. Stop depriving one another, except by agreement for a time that you may devote yourselves to prayer, and come together again lest Satan tempt you because of your lack of self-control.

Discussion Questions

For Better, Not Worse: A One-Sentence Success Story

Testimony Time: Several of you state briefly what you applied from the last session.

For example . . .

- I decoded why my husband suddenly became moody after I said, "We need more income to pay these bills." I realized he heard me putting him down as an inadequate provider.
- I told my husband how much I respect him for working so hard and providing for us as a family.
- I told my wife how much I appreciate that she works outside the home to help financially and recognize that her overall desire is for the home.

HIERARCHY: Respecting His Desire to Provide and Protect—Even Die

1. What Is Going On in This Story?*

Missy complains to Stu, "I can't believe you'd buy into that notion that the man is the breadwinner and defender of the castle. We're equal and don't you forget it. And while I'm expressing things that upset me about you, I can't believe you walked ahead of me to the car. I almost fell on the ice. What if I had broken my leg? Would your insurance cover me? Plus, why did you let our teen son make fun of me and say that I looked like a calf on ice? Stu, you are pretty low on the 'What-it-means-to-be-a-human-being scale.' " Stu is crushed. He is put down for who he is and he closes off his spirit and walks away from her, refusing to talk.

- What does Stu need?
- Does Missy decode this?
- As a husband, in the past what would your response have been to Missy?
- As a wife, in the past what would your response have been to Stu's response?
- Explain how this leads to *the Crazy Cycle*.

2. Right or Responsibility?

Ephesians 5:23–24 says, "For the husband is the head of the wife, as Christ also is the head of the church, He Himself being the Savior of the body. But as the church is subject (the Greek word

_____

_____

_____

_____

_____

_____

_____

_____

_____

is hupotasso) to Christ, so also the wives ought to be to their husbands in everything." This verse teaches that the husband is "the head." Is this a right or a responsibility? What is the difference?

Since being the head entails dying for one's wife like Christ died for the church, is it accurate to say the Bible is stressing a husband's responsibilities, and not his rights, over his wife? Why or why not?

3. Disrespect Breaks a Husband's Spirit

As a young couple struggling in the ministry, E. V. Hill came home one evening to a dark home but Jane, his wife, was standing in the dining room with candlelight and a hot dinner! Wow! She had prepared this for the two of them. Before sitting down he decided to wash his hands in the bathroom. As he flipped on the lights, they did not come on. He realized the electricity had been turned off. Returning to Jane, she began to cry. "You work so hard, and we're trying," said Jane, "but it's pretty rough. I didn't have enough money to pay the light bill. I didn't want you to know about it, so I thought we would just eat by candlelight."

Dr. Hill described his wife's words with intense emotion: "She could have said, 'I've never been in this situation before. I was reared in the home of Dr. Caruthers, and we never had our lights cut off.' She could have broken my spirit; she could have ruined me; she could have demoralized me. But instead she said, 'Somehow or other we'll get these lights back on. But tonight, let's eat by candlelight'" (Dr. Dobson's monthly newsletter, Feb. 1995, page 3).

What happens in the heart of a husband who is viewed by his wife as not being a good-enough provider?

How sensitive was E. V. Hill to the thought that his wife might not respect his desire and ability to provide for her?

AUTHORITY: Desire to be Strong and to Lead (to Make Decisions)
4. What Is Going On in This Story?*

A stalemate had arisen between Missy and Stu. Should they put money into a private school for the kids or hire an in-home teacher? Missy told Stu to evaluate the alternatives. As Stu got into it, he favored spending the money on private schooling. When he said this, something in Missy fa-

_____

_____

_____

_____

_____

_____

_____

_____

vored hiring an in-home teacher. Tension now existed. Stu said, "Okay, a decision has to be made. Before the fall, either the kids need to be enrolled or we need to hire someone. I'm making the decision in two days." When he decided for private schooling, she reacted saying, "You can't make the decision. We're equal." Stu blew his stack.

- What does Stu need?
- Does Missy decode this?
- As a husband, in the past what would your response have been to Missy?
- As a wife, in the past what would your response have been to Stu?
- How will this lead to *the Crazy Cycle*?

5. Good Managers

What do most Christian men believe God is calling them to do based on 1 Timothy 3:12?

Men, do you agree or disagree with these scriptures, that you must be one who knows how to manage his own household?

6. Markers of Authority

Dr. Deborah Tannen, the great linguist and expert in male and female communication, states that men are taller, more heftily built, and have a lower-pitched voice. She calls these "markers of authority." Women are generally smaller, slighter, and have a higher-pitched voice.

What do you think of the idea that God created man with these "markers of authority" to enable him to carry out his responsibilities to protect and provide?

7. Leadership 101

Agree or disagree? Since the husband is called upon to manage his household and even die for his wife and family, then he is at least 51 percent responsible for the marriage.

Leadership 101 says that when a person has the primary responsibility, that person must have the primary authority. In business a person is set up for failure when told to be responsible, but then hears, "But you don't have any authority to carry that out."

_____

_____

_____

_____

_____

_____

_____

_____

INSIGHT: Respecting His Desire to Analyze and Counsel
8. What Is Going On in This Story?*

Stu says to Missy, "I hesitate to bring this up, but I sometimes feel when you are with your friends, you bad-mouth others who have made you mad. You are discrediting these folks. Missy, you are too good of a person to get caught up in all this gossip and backbiting." Missy yells, "You are right about being too good of a person. Who do you think you are to tell me anything? Don't try to fix me. Women today are the better sex. We listen better, we understand better, and we empathize better. You insult me." She heads to the garage, slams the door, and leaves.

Men, how would you respond to Missy's self-righteous attitude? How do these attitudes affect a man's willingness to give insight?

9. Eve Was Deceived

Just as a man has unique vulnerabilities because of his maleness (i.e., visual sexual temptations—2 Samuel 11:2; Matthew 5:28), a woman has unique vulnerabilities because of her femaleness.

We read about such a vulnerability in 1 Timothy 2:14, ". . . it was not Adam who was deceived, but the woman being deceived, fell into transgression."

What were the consequences when Eve was misled by another voice and her own feelings?

10. Her Invalid Feelings

A wife wrote: "I know the Lord created me an emotional being and that's okay. But that I can be misled by my feelings was a 'new' thought for me."

Women, think of a time when you were misled by your feelings, and if appropriate, share with the group.

What would happen if your husband remarked, "Honey, I know you want me to validate your feelings, but I don't believe your feelings are valid on this specific matter"?

How does Matthew 18:16, where Jesus says that every fact must be confirmed by two or three witnesses (not every feeling be validated), apply to this situation?

_____

_____

_____

_____

_____

_____

_____

_____

_____

RELATIONSHIP: Appreciating His Desire For Shoulder-to-Shoulder Friendship

11. What Is Going On in This Story?*

In front of Stu, Missy told the marriage counselor, "I don't accept Stu's stupid invitations. He says, 'Let's go to the athletic club to walk and lift weights together.' Or, 'Hey, let's go watch the basketball game.' Or, 'I thought about buying a tandem bike.' But I refuse these requests. We need to work on our relationship. Communication is everything. If our relationship is going to make it, we need to be talking. Instead, he wants to play."

How are Missy and Stu defining differently how they feel they should work on their relationship? Are they both right?

12. When Do Men Really Open Up?

Some educators believe boys should not go to school until age ten since up to that time they learn best outside, doing activities, and listening to stories. But get this. Jesus the Master Teacher had twelve men, spending most of his time outside, doing activities, and telling parables. Every man knows his best buddies are those he likes doing activities with shoulder-to-shoulder. Over time, they open up. They don't need to talk a lot, but when together they are energized. Deborah Tannen's research shows that men tend to sit shoulder-to-shoulder and periodically share their thoughts. Women on the other hand need to be face-to-face to talk.

Are men wrong? In her research the two sixteen-year-old boys opened up more than the other men and the women. However, they said very little yet were extremely transparent.

Most men open up after doing activities together, without much talking. What is the application of this to your marriage? Men, share how you relate to this.

13. Shoulder-to-Shoulder Friendship

Song of Solomon 5:16 says, "He is wholly desirable. This is my beloved and this is my friend." Women, think back to your courtship. Do you remember expressing your desire to be with him as your forever friend?

_____

_____

_____

_____

_____

_____

_____

_____

_____

What did he hear? "Wow, she will always be there to cheer me on!" He envisioned you being friendly day after day in the same way you envisioned him emotionally connecting with you day after day.

Though children came and life got busy, did his desire for friendship shoulder-to-shoulder change any more than your desire to talk face-to-face? Discuss.

14. She Likes Me, She Likes Me Not

Feeling exhausted and unloved, a negativity sets in. Some wives become unfriendly in the home. Ask a husband, "Does your wife love you?" He'll answer, "Yes." Then ask him, "Does she like you?" He'll reply, "No, not today."

Read Titus 2:3–4. Why do you think Paul tells the older women to encourage the younger women to love (phileo—friendship love) their husbands?

SEXUALITY: Appreciating His Desire for Sexual Intimacy

15. What Is Going On in This Story?*

Stu got up the courage to tell Missy of his sexual desires. Her retort was, "Well, I'm too tired. Besides, you don't deserve sex. You never talk to me heart to heart." Stu says, "But what am I trying to do right now? When I tell you deep things like this, you come uncorked." Missy continues, "I don't have the need. Besides, the kids take priority right now. What's important is for you to talk to me about things that matter to me and then maybe these other things might happen."

16. His Visual Orientation

Explain how the following verses reveal a man's visual orientation and thus both his joy and struggle.

Proverbs 5:19 As a loving hind and a graceful doe, let her breasts satisfy you at all times; be exhilarated always with her love.

Matthew 5:28 But I say to you that everyone who looks at a woman with lust for her has already committed adultery with her in his heart.

17. Depriving

First Corinthians 7:5 says, "Stop depriving one another, except by agreement for a time, so that you may devote yourselves to prayer, and come together again so that Satan will not tempt you because of your lack of self-control."

What can happen when a husband, or for that matter a wife, is deprived sexually?

18. Getting to a Husband's Heart

Comment on these ideas. Care about your wife's heart and she'll respond sexually. Care about a husband sexually and he'll open his heart and respond to his wife's heart. This begs the question: Who moves first?

What happens when both choose to be mature?

Immediate Application

Write down in the space below one or two things that came to mind during this session that you already know you need to begin applying or practicing this week.

_____

_____

_____

_____

_____

_____

_____

_____

_____

_____

_____

_____

_____

_____

_____

_____

_____

_____

Midweek Devotional

Your Spouse Has Needs Only You Can Fill

Don't be concerned only about your own interests, but also be concerned about the interests of others. Have the same attitude that Christ Jesus had.

—Philippians 2:4–5 GW

You may have heard more than one sermon on today's key verse, usually applied to life in the church with fellow believers. But have you thought about how it applies to your marriage? What better place not to be concerned with only your own agenda; but to be at least equally concerned about your spouse's interests, concerns, hopes, and dreams. Why? What should be your incentive? Love and respect? Yes, but even more fundamental is that you "have the same attitude that Christ Jesus had" (Philippians 2:5).

Of course, this means putting your own needs aside, at least for the moment. It means sacrificing for the sake of the one you decided to spend your life with. Sarah is a great example of doing just that. It is not Sarah's first choice to endure the stress of getting us to the airport and then take another long ride to a faraway city for the next Love & Respect Conference. But Sarah puts her interests aside for the sake of the ministry, for which I am far more thankful than I can express on paper or even in person. To say, "She is invaluable," would be a gross understatement.

And what about Emerson? What is his sacrifice? My obvious main interests in life are studying, writing, and preparing material. One of Sarah's interests (perhaps it is her main interest) is engaging in the well-documented Pinkie pastime of talking, particularly with me. Over the years I have learned to put aside my studying and writing to hear her concerns several times a week, if not daily.

Sarah will tell you that I have truly given of myself to allow her to talk. I have not shut down, saying, "I am the way I am. Deal with it!" (I admit I have had the thought a few times, but God is good, and He has protected me from myself, not to mention my sweet little wife.)

The point of today's key verse is clear: don't just be concerned about your own agenda; think about the interests of others—especially your spouse (see Philippians 2:4). So far, so good, but is there some motivation that would help us do this, besides the fear of feeling guilty if we don't come through? We find a very big clue in verse 5: "Have the same attitude that Christ Jesus had." As the rest of what is called the "kenosis passage" points out, Jesus "emptied himself," putting aside His deity to live among us and meet our deepest need—salvation from our sin (see Philippians 2:6–11).

As you and your spouse seek to imitate your Savior and Lord within marriage, you quickly learn that you both have needs only the other can meet. Could that mean functioning outside your comfort zone and even feeling inadequate? Possibly, but your incentive is that your spouse needs you, no one else. That is not an imposition, it's a compliment worthy of praise to the heavenly Father, because such moments allow you to imitate Jesus and thereby honor Him. Such moments chip away your un-Christlike features as you "let the Spirit renew your thoughts and attitudes" (Ephesians 4:23 NLT).

So the next time you have an opportunity to look to the needs or concerns of your spouse when it is, quite frankly, inconvenient or even a bit painful for you, think about how your new attitude in Christ is helping sand off the rough edges of selfishness. Your spouse has a need only you can fill. Instead of bringing up a lot of reasons why you can't do it, or the things your spouse might do instead, see the situation for what it is. Say to yourself, or even aloud, "Thanks, honey, thanks for the compliment!"

Prayer: Thank the Lord for His invitation to have the same attitude that Christ Jesus had, and for the ways He helps sand away the rough edges of self-interest as you both have opportunities to meet each other's needs for love and respect. Ask Him for the wisdom and humility to always see your spouse's needs as a compliment, not a cause for your complaints. (Also look outside the family, to work, church, and other situations where you can put the needs of others ahead of your own and have your actions come full-circle in various ways.)

Action: During the coming week, practice responding to each other's requests and needs by saying, "Thanks for the compliment." As a reminder to do this, put Post-it notes in strategic places saying, "Have the same attitude that Christ Jesus had."

For more "husband-friendly devotionals that wives truly love," see Emerson's book The Love & Respect Experience (Thomas Nelson, 2011).

SESSION SEVEN

In-Session Guide

Sarah's Practical Application: Part 1
As Your Wife I Feel Loved When...

Closeness: A woman feels close to you **(face to face and heart to heart)** when you:
- hold her hand
- hug her
- are affectionate without sexual intentions

Openness: A woman feels an openness with you **(you are not secretly mad)** when you:
- share your feelings
- tell her about your day and challenges
- talk without harshness, guardedness, or grunting

Understanding: A woman feels you understand her **(empathize with her)** when you:
- listen to her (know when to give advice and when not to solve her problems)
- repeat back what she says so she knows you're listening to her
- express appreciation for her contribution and roles by saying, "I couldn't do your job"

Peacemaking: A woman feels at peace with you **(issues are resolved)** when you:
- admit you are wrong and apologize by saying "I am sorry" (which is a turn-on to a woman)
- keep the relationship up to date, resolve the unresolved, and don't say "forget it"
- pray together after a hurtful time

_____

_____

_____

_____

_____

_____

_____

_____

_____

Loyalty: A woman feels your loyalty **(complete commitment)** when you:
- don't look at other women
- speak only positive things about her before family and friends; no airing of dirty laundry
- do not bring up the "D" word (divorce) but are committed until death do us part

Esteem: A woman feels esteemed by you **(treasured above others)** when you:
- verbally support and honor her in front of the children
- praise her for what she does for you
- value her opinion in the gray areas; not wrong, just different from you

_____

_____

_____

_____

_____

_____

_____

_____

_____

_____

_____

_____

_____

_____

_____

_____

_____

_____

_____

_____

_____

_____

_____

_____

_____

_____

_____

_____

_____

Discussion Questions

For Better, Not Worse: A One-Sentence Success Story

Testimony Time: Several of you state briefly what you applied from the last session.

For example . . .

- I realized as a husband that God calls me to be the head like Christ is the head. I am responsible and need to take those responsibilities more seriously.
- I paid more attention to the sexual temptations that visually bombard men in the culture.
- I did some shoulder-to-shoulder activities with my husband.

1. Share Your Successes

The best way to respect a wife is to love her in ways that are meaningful to her. As Sarah went through the practical application for **C.O.U.P.L.E.**, discuss in the group what you feel, as a couple, are some successful areas for you with regard to loving. Look at the whole list under **C.O.U.P.L.E.** and discuss the positive applications of love that you see in your marriage. Jump in on any item under any of the letters and start talking.

For instance, a wife may share, "My husband still holds my hand when we go for a walk." Or, a husband may share, "My dad had a problem with harshness and I have really tried to be gentle with my wife."

2. Share What You Intend to Improve

In the same manner, share with one another areas that you need to shore up.

For example, a wife may share, "I need to let him know that I need a listening ear instead of making him guess." Or, a husband may share, "I need to be quicker to say, 'I am sorry. Will you forgive me?'" Remember, for the goodwilled and mature husband who intends to move first, his love can motivate his wife's respect.

There is a Love and Respect connection! When a husband commits to **C.O.U.P.L.E.** this can energize his wife to respect his desires related to **C.H.A.I.R.S.**

3. The Love and Respect Connection: His Love (C.O.U.P.L.E.) Motivates Her Respect (C.H.A.I.R.S.)*

Explain why the following connections should work.

1. When a husband lovingly talks with his wife face-to-face (**C**), she will be motivated to respect his desire to do shoulder-to-shoulder activities (**R**).
2. When a husband lovingly opens up with his wife (**O**), that is, meets her need for emotional release, she will be motivated to respect his desire to be sexually intimate (**S**), that is, meet his need for sexual release.
3. When a husband lovingly empathizes with his wife's feelings (**U**), she will be energized to respect his desire to offer helpful counsel to her (**I**).
4. When a husband lovingly resolves issues and seeks to reconcile heart-to-heart with his wife, evidencing a cooperative spirit (**P**), she will want to respect his management (**A**) when the hard decisions need to be made.
5. When a husband lovingly assures his wife of his commitment to her (**L**), she will want to respect his desire to work and achieve outside the home (**C**), even when it takes him away from her more than she wishes.
6. When a husband lovingly honors his wife as his equal (**E**), she will want to respect his desire to be the head who protects and provides (**H**).

If a husband seeks to **C.O.U.P.L.E.** yet his wife is unresponsive, why has he earned the right to appeal to her to be more responsive to him in areas related to **C.H.A.I.R.S**?

Will a goodwilled wife respond to him? Discuss.

Note: To learn more about the connection between C.O.U.P.L.E. and C.H.A.I.R.S. read chapter 8 in Emerson's book The Language of Love & Respect.

Immediate Application

Write down in the space below one or two things that came to mind during this session that you already know you need to begin applying or practicing this week.

_____

_____

_____

_____

_____

_____

_____

_____

_____

_____

_____

Midweek Devotional

Question: What Is Love? Answer: C-O-U-P-L-E

But each one of you must love his wife as he loves himself.

—Ephesians 5:33 NCV

I received an e-mail from Nathan, and he asked: "Husbands are to 'love' their wives. That's their special command. So what is love?" Excellent question. There all kinds of answers, many of them rather flowery, syrupy, and some very romantic. I wrote back to Nathan with what I believe are practical, down-to-earth, biblical instructions on how a husband can spell **love** to his wife, providing six things described in chapters 8 through 14 of my book *Love & Respect*, by using the acronym C-O-U-P-L-E.

- **C:** Closeness. You are seeking to be close—face-to-face—and not just when you want sex (Genesis 2:24). This is the idea behind cleaving.
- **O:** Openness. You are trying to be more open with her, sharing more of your heart and definitely closing off in anger far less often (Colossians 3:19).
- **U:** Understanding. You are pulling back from trying to "fix" her and are listening more, trying to be considerate when she's really upset (1 Peter 3:7).
- **P:** Peacemaking. In order to resolve conflict and be united as a team, you are trying to use the words of power: "Honey, I'm sorry. Will you forgive me?" (Matthew 19:5).
- **L:** Loyalty. You are exerting effort to assure her of your love and your "until death do us part" commitment (Malachi 2:14).
- **E:** Esteem. You are viewing her as your equal before God and honoring and treasuring her as first in importance to you (1 Peter 3:7).

The C-O-U-P-L-E acronym is the first half of *the Energizing Cycle*, which teaches that "his love motivates her respect, her respect motivates his love" (see appendix B, page 275). As Sarah and I receive feedback, we are fairly sure people get it about stopping *the Crazy Cycle*. But we wonder how well husbands and wives are using the ideas in *the Energizing Cycle*. To have a happy, biblically solid marriage, you and your spouse need to do a lot more than just work on stopping *the Crazy Cycle*. And that is where *the Energizing Cycle* comes in. When you keep *the Energizing Cycle* humming, *the Crazy Cycle* stays in its cage and you function as the team God wants you to be.

In this devotional I am suggesting that you and your mate take a few moments to reflect on the love in your marriage. What kinds of loving acts and words are happening? Right here, one or both of you may conclude that I am putting all the pressure on the husband (these six things are, after all, what he is supposed to be doing to connect with his wife). But that's not what I have in mind at all.

Using the C-O-U-P-L-E acronym, I want you to look for positives and plusses, not negatives and minuses. For many of us, it is all too easy to see the cup half empty instead of looking for the acts and words that make it half full, and often more. As a wife, guard against only seeing what your husband is overlooking; instead, appreciate his loving words and actions. As a husband, guard against feeling that you can never be good enough; instead, receive encouragement from how you have been obeying God's command to act lovingly: "Each one of you also must love his wife as he loves himself" (Ephesians 5:33).

What is love? It is not a noun but a verb. It is something a husband does—in word and deed. One analogy is to picture the word LOVE, carved from a single block of beautiful oak or maple, bit by bit, day by day. Your marriage is like that block of wood. Love doesn't just happen; you have to work at it, and many husbands do. Remember, looking at the positive does not mean we are being naïve about the negative, but if any team looks only at its losses and never at its victories, it will grow discouraged. Winners need to celebrate their victories as an incentive to taste even more. Rejoice!

Prayer: Thank the Lord for the love that is evident in your marriage. Thank Him for where biblical love is being spelled out in your marriage: Closeness, Openness, Understanding, Peacemaking, Loyalty, and Esteem.

Action: Explore different ways to share love together. Need specifics? Choose from the sixty ideas located at the end of each chapter in the C-O-U-P-L-E section of *Love & Respect*. For example, just as this devotional encourages you to do, start by talking about the positive, loving things that are happening in your marriage, then go on from there.

For more "husband-friendly devotionals that wives truly love," see Emerson's book The Love & Respect Experience *(Thomas Nelson, 2011).*

In-Session Guide

Sarah's Practical Application: Part 2

As Your Husband I Feel Respected When...

Conquest: A man feels you appreciate his pursuits in his field **(his desire to work and achieve)** when you:

- thank him for going to work every day for the family
- cheer his successes whether in business or in sports
- ask him to talk about his dreams

Hierarchy: A man feels you appreciate his position as overseer **(his desire to protect and provide and even die for you)** when you:

- say to him, "I really do look up to you for feeling responsible for me"
- tell him that you are deeply touched by the thought that he would die for you
- praise his commitment to provide, i.e., "bring home the bacon"

Authority: A man feels you appreciate his power on your behalf **(his desire to be strong, to lead, and to make decisions)** when you:

- tell him he's strong as you squeeze his muscle (it's symbolic)
- praise his good decisions
- honor his authority in front of the kids and differ with him in private

Insight: A man feels you appreciate his perspective and proposals **(his desire to analyze and counsel)** when you:

- thank him for his advice and knowledge
- let him fix things and applaud his solution orientation
- tell him upfront you need "an ear" to listen and not a solution

Relationship: A man feels you value his partnership and pastimes **(his desire for a shoulder-to-shoulder friendship)** when you:

- tell him you like him
- do recreational activities with him, or watch him do them
- encourage alone time for him; this energizes him to reconnect with you later

Sexuality: A man feels you appreciate his passions and pleasures **(his desire for sexual intimacy)** when you:

- initiate periodically
- respond more often
- let him acknowledge his sexual temptations without shaming him

Discussion Questions

For Better, Not Worse: A One-Sentence Success Story

Testimony Time: Did anyone experience *the Energizing Cycle*? That is, did your loving actions as a husband (related to **C.O.U.P.L.E.**) motivate your wife's respectful responses (related to **C.H.A.I.R.S.**)?

For example . . .

Husbands . . .

- Did your closeness face-to-face motivate your wife's desire to be shoulder-to-shoulder with you?
- Did your understanding motivate your wife's desire to respond more positively to your insight?
- Did your attempt to cooperate as a peacemaker motivate your wife to respond to your leadership and authority?

Wives, feel free to participate in this discussion.

Couples, please share specific examples of how you saw this connection work this past week.

There is a Love and Respect connection. When a wife respects **C.H.A.I.R.S.** this energizes the husband to commit to **C.O.U.P.L.E.**

1. Share Your Successes

The best way to love a husband is to respect him in ways that are meaningful to him. As Sarah went through the practical application for **C.H.A.I.R.S.**, discuss in the group what you feel, as a couple, are some successful areas for you with regard to respecting. Look at the whole list under **C.H.A.I.R.S.** and discuss the positive applications of respect that you see in your marriage. Jump in on any item under any of the letters and start talking.

For instance, a husband may share, "My wife tells me often that she appreciates my hard work for the family." Or, a wife may share, "I have been committed through the years to refrain from saying anything negative about my husband in front of the children since that can be so demeaning of

_____

_____

_____

_____

_____

_____

_____

_____

_____

his leadership, and he has done the same toward me."

2. Share What You Intend to Improve

In the same manner, share with one another areas that you intend to shore up.

For example, a husband may share, "I need to refrain from giving her a solution, when she isn't asking for a solution but for understanding." Or, a wife may share, "I need to be more friendly and positive."

3. The Love and Respect Connection: Her Respect (C.H.A.I.R.S.) Motivates His Love (C.O.U.P.L.E.)*

Explain why the following connections should work.

1. When a wife respects her husband's friendship shoulder-to-shoulder (**R**), he will be motivated to lovingly talk to her face-to-face (**C**).
2. When a wife respects her husband's desire to be sexually intimate (**S**), he will be motivated to be lovingly open with her (**O**).
3. When a wife respects her husband's helpful counsel (**I**), he will be energized to lovingly empathize with her feelings (**U**) when she tells him she needs a listening ear.
4. When a wife respects her husband's desire to manage the family (**A**), especially when the hard decisions need to be made, he will want to lovingly resolve issues and seek to reconcile heart-to-heart with her (**P**), evidencing a cooperative spirit, during the daily decisions.
5. When a wife respects her husband's desire to work and achieve outside the home (**C**), he will want to lovingly reassure her of his commitment to her (**L**).
6. When a wife respects her husband's desire to be the head as protector and provider (**H**), he will want to lovingly honor her as his equal (**E**).

If a wife seeks to respect **C.H.A.I.R.S.** yet her husband is unresponsive, why has she earned the right to appeal to him to be more responsive to her in areas related to **C.O.U.P.L.E.**? Will a good-willed husband respond to her? Discuss.

Note: To learn more about the connection between C.H.A.I.R.S. and C.O.U.P.L.E. read chapter 8 in Emerson's book The Language of Love & Respect.

_____

_____

_____

_____

_____

_____

_____

_____

_____

Immediate Application

Write down in the space below one or two things that came to mind during this session that you already know you need to begin applying or practicing this week.

Midweek Devotional

Question: What Is Respect? Answer. C-H-A-I-R-S

And the wife must respect her husband.

—Ephesians 5:33 NIV

The e-mail from Wendy stated: "I feel the biggest question or concern women have is, what is respect?" I wrote back to say I heartily agree; it is, in fact, the question wives ask me most. Not surprisingly, I answered it in much the same way I answered Nathan when he e-mailed to ask, what is love? Respect, for a man, is not rocket science. I described six practical, biblical ways that a wife can express respect for her husband in chapters 15 through 21 of *Love & Respect*, using the acronym C-H-A-I-R-S.

- **C:** Conquest. You are seeking to recognize and thank him for his desire to work and provide for his family (Genesis 2:15).
- **H:** Hierarchy. You are trying to thank him for his desire to be responsible in protecting and providing (Ephesians 5:23).
- **A:** Authority. You are trying to pull back from subverting his leadership, albeit innocently, and are seeking ways to acknowledge his desire to lead and serve (Ephesians 5:22).
- **I:** Insight. You are endeavoring to appreciate his desire to analyze and counsel by listening to the ideas and advice he offers (1 Timothy 2:14).
- **R:** Relationship. You are valuing his desire for you to be his friend and stand shoulder to shoulder with him (Titus 2:4; Song of Solomon 5:1).
- **S:** Sexuality. You are seeking to respond to him, appreciating his desire for sexual intimacy that only you can meet (Proverbs 5:19; 1 Corinthians 7:5).

The C-H-A-I-R-S acronym is the other half of *the Energizing Cycle*: her respect motivates his love. As I often share when speaking or writing, respect for the husband is a harder sell than love for the wife mainly because so many wives feel "he is failing to love me as he ought to, so he has to earn my respect." Of course, that is just the point. He doesn't have to earn her respect any more than she has to earn his love. Both are to be unconditional. God commands a wife to put on respect independent of who her husband is (1 Peter 3:1–2; Ephesians 5:33), just as God commands a husband to put on love regardless of his wife's lovability (Ephesians 5:25, 33; Hosea 3:1).

But what about Wendy's question: what, exactly, is respect? How does a wife show it? Note that all of the principles taught in C-H-A-I-R-S include the idea that the wife is to appreciate her husband's desire to succeed at work, protect and provide, serve and lead, analyze and counsel, enjoy her friendship, and engage in sexual lovemaking. The respectful wife seeks to honor her husband's desires, not because he is perfectly honoring her desires but because she intends to obey God's call to give him unconditional respect. She realizes this really isn't about her husband; it is God's command to her as a wife (Ephesians 5:33).

As you engage in this devotional together, take a few moments to reflect on the respect in your marriage. Using the C-H-A-I-R-S acronym, look for the positives and pluses, not the negatives and minuses. Husband, guard against making this an "I gotcha!" game by just looking for ways you aren't getting proper respect at all times. Instead, be thankful for your wife's respectful words and actions. And wife, don't feel defeated if showing respect may sometimes seem awkward. Like love, respect doesn't just happen. Like love, respect is something to be carved out a little bit each day as the wife obeys God's command "And the wife must respect her husband" (Ephesians 5:33).

According to Dale Carnegie, "Truly respecting others is the bedrock of motivation." When a wife truly respects a husband's desires as outlined in C-H-A-I-R-S, most likely he will be motivated to truly love her as outlined in C-O-U-P-L-E, and *the Energizing Cycle* will hum!

Prayer: Thank the Lord for the respect that is present in your marriage. Ask Him for wisdom and guidance in appreciating and sharing the desires He built into men: to work and achieve, to protect and provide, to serve and to lead, to analyze and counsel, to enjoy shoulder-to-shoulder friendship, and to enjoy sexual intimacy.

Action: Use the suggestions at the end of the *Love & Respect* chapters on C-H-A-I-R-S, thirty-eight ideas in all, to explore and expand the concept of respect in your marriage.

For more "husband-friendly devotionals that wives truly love," see Emerson's book The Love & Respect Experience (Thomas Nelson, 2011).

In-Session Guide

The Rewarded Cycle: Part 1

A. The Rewarded Cycle Rewards Forever, Resulting in the Unending First

_____.

Revelation 22:12 Behold, I am coming quickly, and **My reward is with Me**, to render to every man according to what he has done.

James 1:12 Blessed is a man who perseveres under trial; for once he has been approved, **he will receive the crown of life,** which the Lord has promised to those who love Him.

2 John 1:8 Watch yourselves, that you might not lose what we have accomplished, but **that you may receive a full reward.**

Mark 12:19-25 Teacher, Moses wrote for us that if a man's brother dies, and leaves behind a wife, and leaves no child, his brother should take the wife, and raise up offspring to his brother. There were seven brothers; and the first took a wife, and died, leaving no offspring. And the second one took her, and died, leaving behind no offspring; and the third likewise; and so all seven left no offspring. Last of all the woman died also. In the resurrection, when they rise again, **which one's wife will she be? For all seven had her as a wife."** Jesus said to them, "Is this not the reason you are mistaken, that you do not understand the Scriptures, or the power of God? **For when they rise from the dead, they neither marry, nor are given in marriage, but are like angels in heaven.**

Revelation 21:9 Come here, I shall show you the bride, **the wife of the Lamb.**

Unconditional Respect is Rewarded.

Ephesians 6:7-8 With good will render service, **as to the Lord,** and not to men, **knowing that whatever good thing each one does, this he will receive back from the Lord,** whether slave or free.

_____

_____

_____

_____

_____

_____

_____

_____

_____

Ephesians 5:22 Wives, [be subject] to your own husbands, **as to the Lord.**

Ephesians 5:33 ... and the wife must see to it that she **respects her husband.**

2 Corinthians 5:10 For we must all appear before the judgment seat of Christ, that each one may be **recompensed** for his deeds in the body, according to what he has done, whether good or bad.

Unconditional Love is Rewarded.

Matthew 5:46 For if you **love** those who **love** you, what **reward** have you? Do not even the tax-gatherers do the same?

Luke 6:32-34 And if you **love** those who **love** you, what **credit** is [that] to you? For even sinners **love** those who **love** them. And if you do good to those who do good to you, what **credit** is [that] to you? For even sinners do the same. And if you lend to those from whom you expect to receive, what **credit** is [that] to you? Even sinners lend to sinners, in order to receive back the same [amount].

1 Peter 2:20 For what **credit** is there if, when you sin and are harshly treated, you endure it with patience? But if when you do what is right and suffer [for it] you patiently endure it, this [finds] **favor with God.**

B. The Rewarded Cycle Deepens and Demonstrates Our Love and Reverence for Christ as We Do This " _____ " Christ.

"You did it to Me" principle.

Matthew 25:37-40 Then the righteous will answer Him, saying, "Lord, when did we see You hungry, and feed You, or thirsty, and give You drink? And when did we see You a stranger, and invite You in, or naked, and clothe You? And when did we see You sick, or in prison, and come to You?" And the King will answer and say to them, "Truly I say to you, **to the extent that** you did it to one of these brothers of Mine, [even] the least [of them], **you did it to Me.**"

Matthew 25:45 Then He will answer them, saying, "Truly I say to you, **to the extent that** you did not do it to one of the least of these, **you did not do it to Me.**"

_____

_____

_____

_____

_____

_____

_____

_____

Unconditional love reveals a husband's imitation of Christ and thus love for Christ. He shows his love for Christ as he loves his wife.

Ephesians 5:2 And **walk in love, just as Christ** also loved you, and gave Himself up for us, an offering and a sacrifice to God as a fragrant aroma.

Ephesians 5:25 Husbands, **love your wives, just as Christ** also loved the church and gave Himself up for her …

Ephesians 5:29 For no one ever hated his own flesh, but nourishes and cherishes it, **just as Christ** also [does] the church …

1 John 4:21 And this commandment we have from Him, that **the one who loves God should love his brother also.**

Unconditional respect reveals a wife's reverence for Christ. She shows her reverence for Christ as she respects her husband.

Titus 2:3 Older women likewise are to be **reverent in their behavior** …

Ephesians 5:21 And be subject to one another in the fear of Christ ["**reverence,**" NIV].

Ephesians 5:22 Wives, [be subject] to your own husbands, **as to the Lord.**

Ephesians 5:33 … and the wife must see to it that she **respects her husband.**

Ephesians 6:7 With good will render service, **as to the Lord,** and not to men.

Titus 2:4-5 That they may encourage the young women to **love their husbands** [phileo] … that the word of God may not be **dishonored.**

_____

_____

_____

_____

_____

_____

_____

_____

_____

_____

_____

_____

_____

_____

Discussion Questions

For Better, Not Worse: A One-Sentence Success Story

Testimony Time: Did any of you experience *the Energizing Cycle*? That is, did your respectful actions (related to **C.H.A.I.R.S.**) motivate your husband's loving responses (related to **C.O.U.P.L.E.**)?

For example, wives . . .

- Did your shoulder-to-shoulder time with him motivate your husband's desire for closeness face-to-face?

- Did your positive response to his insights motivate your husband's desire to be more understanding of you?

- Did your positive response to his leadership and authority motivate your husband's desire to cooperate as a peacemaker?

Husbands, please feel free to participate in this discussion.

Couples, share specific examples of how you saw this connection work in the past week.

1. The Little Engine That Could

Imagine if you were offered five million dollars to be loving and respectful toward one another for five weeks. The catch is, a film crew would follow you around 24/7 to see if you showed any signs of hostility and disdain. For five million dollars, would you refrain from being unloving and disrespectful?

This begs the question: Do we lack the ability to be loving or respectful or do we lack the incentive? Discuss.

If one decides to "rationalize" that they can't do this, this is comparable to "rational lies." We could all learn something from *The Little Engine That Could*: "I think I can, I think I can, I think I can."

2. Some Spouses Won't Respond*

True or false? Sometimes a wife will not show respect for her husband no matter how hard he tries to show her unconditional love.

_____

_____

_____

_____

_____

_____

_____

_____

But, can he continue to show unconditional love?

True or false? Sometimes a husband will not show love for his wife, no matter how hard she tries to unconditionally respect him.

But, can she continue to show unconditional respect?

In the eyes of God, no act of love and respect is wasted, even if one's spouse is unresponsive. Everything matters! What does this mean to you?

3. The Rewarded Cycle

When a spouse does not respond, you have the potential of getting on **the Rewarded Cycle**, which is summed up like this:

> *HIS LOVE BLESSES REGARDLESS OF HER RESPECT*
> *HER RESPECT BLESSES REGARDLESS OF HIS LOVE*

Do you believe God blesses or rewards unconditional love and respect? Why or why not?

4. The Lord Rewards*

Ephesians 6:8 says, "You know that the Lord will reward each one for whatever good they do, whether they are slave or free" (NIV). What do you think Paul means by "the Lord will reward each one"?

This truth applies to all believers, and especially to what Paul had just written earlier in Ephesians 5 about the married. Share your thoughts on the following statement: If you love your wife who is disrespectful or respect your husband who is unloving, there is a cha-ching effect in Heaven.

5. The Unending First Moment

On pages 273–74 of Emerson's book entitled *Love & Respect*, we read:

Envision the scene as believers ascend into Heaven and stand before Christ. To one husband He says, "Well done. You've put on love toward your disrespectful wife. You are about to receive back every act of love you did toward her." To a wife He says, "Well done. You've put on respect toward your unloving husband. I watched. You are about to be rewarded for every act of respect."

_____

_____

_____

_____

_____

_____

_____

_____

_____

Next, Jesus directs you to enter the place called Paradise (see Luke 23:43). He has brought you "safely to His heavenly kingdom" (2 Timothy 4:18). As you enter with Jesus, you experience a holy rush. "You stand in the presence of His glory, blameless with great joy" (Jude 24). At that moment, unexpectedly, you behold a gift of such great value you gasp a holy "Ahhh!" What you behold is beyond anything you could imagine. Suddenly, instantly, you are enveloped by love and glory. You are literally "in glory" never to leave (Colossians 3:4).

Not only will you be overwhelmed by that first moment, but that first moment will last forever.

In your own words, describe how incredible you think glory will be.

Consider how remarkable it is that God will reward a person forever and ever who chooses to put on love or respect for many decades, a mere blink of the eye! For the person who says, "It isn't worth it for me to love or respect," is this person a true believer in Christ and Paradise to come?

If this person is a believer, discuss why they might say such a thing, and how you might respond to them.

6. The Desire: To Touch the Heart of God

When you love or respect unconditionally regardless of the outcome, you are following God and His will for you. You aren't primarily loving your wife or respecting your husband for what it can do to improve your marriage. Your real desire is to touch the heart of God.

In the long run, husbands and wives should be practicing Love and Respect principles first and foremost out of a desire to obey Christ and His command in Ephesians 5:33. The believer obeys in order to affect the Lord Jesus and to hear from Him, "Well done, good and faithful servant." Do you agree or disagree?

If you agree, is this mere intellectual assent or do you find that you have a desire to touch Christ's heart and to hear, "Well done"?

Immediate Application

Write down in the space below one or two things that came to mind during this session that you already know you need to begin applying or practicing this week.

_____

_____

_____

_____

_____

_____

_____

_____

_____

Midweek Devotional

To Overcome the Past, Focus on the Prize

Forgetting the past and looking forward to what lies ahead, I press on to reach the end of the race and receive the heavenly prize, for which God, through Christ Jesus, is calling us.

—Philippians 3:13–14 NLT

We are living in a time and culture that is obsessed with winning. As one Indiana high school basketball coach put it, "Oh, Hoosier basketball fans love you—whether you win or tie."

He said it tongue in cheek, of course, but the point is well made. In any endeavor, losing is not really permitted. If you lose, especially if you get on a losing streak, people label you "loser." When I got a chance to speak to the New York Giants players and their coaches, wives, and girlfriends about Love & Respect, I was able to chat afterward with head coach Tom Coughlin, who shared with me about enduring some rough stretches before the Giants became Super Bowl champions. We discussed a lot of the problems he had faced: pressure from the press and being hounded by fanatical fans, especially during losing streaks. As we talked, he mentioned that in the NFL coaches are hired and fired like flies swatted on the wall. If you don't win, "So long!"

Thinking I might glean some wisdom to share with Love & Respect couples, I asked, "How do you deal with adversity?" His answer was immediate, spoken with conviction: "You keep your eye on the prize."

Tom lives by his "eye on the prize" credo and preaches it constantly to his players and assistant coaches. When pressure mounts and difficulties multiply, you focus on the big picture and ultimate goal. Tom became head coach of the Giants in 2004, and in a town like New York nothing will do but winning the Super Bowl. Despite being the target of withering criticism and cynicism, the Giants improved each year, kept making the playoffs, and finally, on February 3, 2008, the Super Bowl championship was theirs as they upset the heavily favored New England Patriots, 17–14.

A nice sports story, you may be thinking, but exactly what does it have to do with my marriage? Quite a bit—maybe everything. You and your spouse are a team, and like any other team you have your wins and your losses. Sometimes adversity seems to hit from within and without, and you go on a losing streak. What then?

It helps to have some extra motivation to deal with setbacks, and we find it in today's key verse: Philippians 3:13–14. If anyone knew something about dealing with adversity, it was Paul the apostle. He was hounded by those who hated him, rejected when he preached Christ, and even stoned and left for dead, but he pressed on, with his eye on the prize. And what was the prize? Not a Super Bowl ring, but a crown of righteousness awarded at the judgment seat of Christ (2 Timothy 4:8).

In basketball-crazy Indiana, high school coaches may be loved only if they "win or tie," but because of your faith in Christ, you are loved, *win or lose*. You and your spouse can press on, knowing that something glorious awaits you if you persevere. No matter what form adversity takes, no matter what the setback might be, *do not see yourself as a loser.* Your race is not over. You have another day to run.

In a letter to the sports-happy Corinthians, Paul observes: "All athletes are disciplined in their training. They do it to win a prize that will fade away, but we do it for an eternal prize" (1 Corinthians 9:25 NLT). The question for every Love & Respect couple is, how important, really, is that eternal prize? When you fail to love or respect and *the Crazy Cycle* roars into action, what will you do? Become your own worst critics, because this Love & Respect thing seems just too difficult? Not if you take the long view. Marriage is not a fifty-yard dash; it is part of the marathon all Christ followers run. As Paul says, forget the past with its setbacks and its losses, and press on. The prize is waiting.

Prayer: Ask the Lord to help you overcome the pain of the past, real as it still may be, as you focus on heaven's prize. Ask Him for the courage and perseverance to keep your eye on the prize—His upward call in Christ Jesus. Thank the Father that He loves you—win, lose, or tie.

Action: Agree together that when setbacks occur, you will say to each other, "Forget yesterday's loss. Let's focus on today's opportunity, because of tomorrow's prize."

For more "husband-friendly devotionals that wives truly love," see Emerson's book The Love & Respect Experience *(Thomas Nelson, 2011).*

In-Session Guide

The Rewarded Cycle: Part 2

C. The Rewarded Cycle Reveals Our Inner Freedom and _____ of Spirit.

My_____ is my responsibility. This reveals who I am. You do not cause me to be the way I am; you reveal the way I am.

Mark 7:21-23 For from within, out of the heart of men, proceed the evil thoughts, fornications, thefts, murders, adulteries, deeds of coveting and wickedness, as well as deceit, sensuality, envy, slander, pride and foolishness. **All these evil things proceed from within** and defile the man.

Love reveals the husband's freedom of spirit and maturity.

Galatians 5:13-14 For you were called to **freedom,** brethren; only do not turn your freedom into an opportunity for the flesh, but through **love serve one another.** For the whole Law is fulfilled in one word, in the statement, "You shall **love** your neighbor as yourself."

Respect reveals the wife's freedom of spirit and maturity.

1 Peter 2:16-17 Act as free men, and do not use your freedom as a covering for evil, but [use it] as bondslaves of God. **Honor all men;** love the brotherhood, fear God, **honor the king.**

1 Peter 2:18 Servants, be submissive to your masters with all **respect, not only to those who are good and gentle, but also to those who are unreasonable.**

1 Peter 3:1-2 In the same way, you wives … **respectful behavior.**

Romans 12:10 … **give preference to one another in honor** …

1 Corinthians 12:23-24 … and those members of the body, **which we deem less honorable, on these we bestow more abundant honor** … But God has [so] composed the body, giving more abundant honor to that member which lacked.

D. The Rewarded Cycle Leaves a Legacy, Revealing That We Are a Good Example to Others.

Unconditional love shows the husband an example. The best thing a father can do for his children is love their mother.

1 Timothy 4:12 in … love … show yourself an example of those who believe.

Unconditional respect shows the wife an example. The best thing a mother can do for her children is respect their father.

1 Timothy 6:1-2 … **regard** their own … **as worthy of all honor** so that the name of God and our doctrine **may not be spoken against** … And … **not be disrespectful** to them because they are brethren, but let them serve them all the more, because those who partake of the benefit are believers and beloved. Teach and preach these principles.

Titus 2:5 … being subject to their own husbands, **that the word of God may not be dishonored.**

E. The Rewarded Cycle Reveals We Are Winning Our Spouse the Wise Way.

Unconditional respect can win your husband.

1 Peter 3:1-2 In the same way, you wives, be submissive to your own husbands so that even if any [of them] are disobedient to the word, they may be **won** without a word by the behavior of their wives, as they observe your chaste **and respectful behavior.**

1 Peter 3:15-16 But sanctify Christ as Lord in your hearts, always [being] ready to make a defense to everyone who asks you to give an account for the hope that is in you, yet with gentleness and **reverence:** and keep a good conscience so that in the thing in which you are slandered, those who revile your good behavior in Christ may be **put to shame.**

1 Corinthians 7:16a For how do you know, O wife, whether you will **save your husband?**

Unconditional love can win your wife.

Hosea 3:1 Then the Lord said to me, "Go again, **love a woman who is loved by her husband, yet an adulteress,** even as the Lord loves the sons of Israel, though they turn to other gods and love raisin cakes."

1 Corinthians 7:16b Or how do you know, O husband, whether you will **save your wife?**

_____

_____

_____

_____

_____

_____

_____

_____

Discussion Questions

For Better, Not Worse: A One-Sentence Success Story

Testimony Time: Several of you state briefly what you applied from the last session.

For example . . .

- I envisioned heaven and the glory that is coming at that unending first moment. The world meant less to me.
- I thought, "All I have to do is put on love and respect in my marriage and God will reward me throughout eternity. Talk about incentive!"
- I confirmed in myself that I am capable (and expected) to still love and respect my spouse unconditionally, no matter his or her response.

1. Marriage Is a Tool and Test*

In His parable of the sheep and the goats, Jesus teaches us to do what we do as to Him (Matthew 25:31–40). Ephesians 5:22 tells wives to submit to their husbands "as to the Lord." Ephesians 5:25 tells husbands to love their wives "just as Christ also loved the church." Paul is teaching husbands and wives that in marriage the true believer is always conscious of Christ. Ultimately one loves or respects because of their love and reverence for Christ.

How does the idea that your marriage is a tool and test to deepen and demonstrate your love and reverence for Christ impact your behavior?

2. In Between You and Jesus

As a husband, you are called upon to love Christ. Periodically, your wife walks between you and Jesus. Your love for Christ should spill over onto your wife as love for her.

If you do not love your wife, what does this reveal about your relationship to Christ?

As a wife, you are called upon to reverence Christ. Periodically, your husband walks between you and Jesus. Your reverence for Christ should spill over onto your husband as respect for him.

If you are not respecting your husband, what does this reveal about your relationship to Christ?

_____

_____

_____

_____

_____

_____

_____

_____

3. Beyond the Shoulder of Your Spouse Stands Christ*

In the ultimate sense, your marriage has nothing to do with your spouse. It has everything to do with your relationship to Jesus Christ. You practice love or respect because beyond your spouse, you picture—with the eyes of faith—Jesus Christ standing there.

How does this biblical reality and imagery encourage you?

4. Pink and Blue Make Purple

The Bible says in Genesis 1:27, "God created man in His own image, in the image of God He created him; male and female He created them." In other words, both male and female reflect the image of God on earth.

Some contend that Jesus the Lover is the image of God on earth. After all, Jesus wants us to be **c**lose to Him, **o**pen to Him, **u**nderstanding of Him, at **p**eace with Him, **l**oyal to Him, and **e**steeming of Him (**C.O.U.P.L.E.**). Some think Jesus is pink and therefore the desires and nature of women best reflect the image of God on earth.

But wait!

Christ the Lord is the **c**onquering king, is **h**ead over all, was given all **a**uthority in heaven and earth, has all wisdom, knowledge and **i**nsight, will **r**elate to us on His terms, and is planting a **s**eed that will be born again into His eternal family (**C.H.A.I.R.S.**). Christ the Lord is blue. Christ the Lord reflects the desires and nature of men.

So to speak, Jesus the Lover is pink and Christ the Lord is blue, but when pink and blue are blended we get purple, the color of royalty, the color of God. Together husband and wife reflect Jesus the Christ, our Loving Lord!

God is not pink. God is not blue. God is purple! Together, as husband and wife they reflect the image of God.

For this reason, when a husband and wife marry and become one, they can and should reflect purple, the whole image of God on earth.

What do you think about this?

Discuss how this could affect you as a couple and how you come across to others.

_____

_____

_____

_____

_____

_____

_____

_____

5. My Response Is My Responsibility*

Suppose Sarah is the one at fault. She is being disrespectful. I have a "right" to feel hurt, angry, depressed. But if I do, I am right back in the victim mind-set again. No matter who is at fault, I can't expect Sarah to heal my hurts or comfort me. My only real comfort will come from my Lord and trusting Him with my situation. Like anyone else, I must grasp a key Love and Respect principle and never let go: No matter how depressing or irritating my spouse might be . . .

My response is my responsibility.

Do you fully believe that your response is your responsibility? What happens when you make your spouse responsible for your response?

Immediate Application

Write down in the space below one or two things that came to mind during this session that you already know you need to begin applying or practicing this week.

_____

_____

_____

_____

_____

_____

_____

_____

_____

_____

_____

_____

_____

_____

_____

_____

_____

_____

_____

_____

_____

_____

_____

_____

Final Devotional

Look! Just Over Your Spouse's Shoulder! It's Jesus!

I tell you the truth, whatever you did for one of the least of these brothers of mine, you did for me.

—Matthew 25:40 NIV

As we come to the last session of a Love & Respect conference, we close with *the Rewarded Cycle*—the very heart and soul of the Love & Respect Connection. And why is it the heart and soul? Because it teaches husbands and wives this all-important truth:

In the ultimate sense, your marriage has nothing to do with your spouse.

It has everything to do with your relationship to Jesus Christ.

The scriptural basis for this statement is Jesus' parable of the last judgment (Matthew 25:31–46). Those deemed righteous ask, "Lord, when did we see you hungry and feed you, or thirsty and give you something to drink? When did we see you a stranger and invite you in, or needing clothes and clothe you? When did we see you sick or in prison and go visit you?" (vv. 37–39). The King answers the righteous and says, "I tell you the truth, whatever you did for one of the least of these brothers of mine, you did for me" (v. 40).

The audience quickly sees the application to them: whatever I do for my spouse, I do for Christ as well. A husband's unconditional love for his wife reveals his love for Christ. If love for her is missing, so is love for Christ. A wife's unconditional respect for her husband reveals her reverence for Christ. If respect for him is missing, so is reverence for Christ.

All of us must make the personal application. Jesus is saying, Emerson, look at me. This isn't about Sarah. She may not deserve love—that's not the point. You show love to Sarah in order to show Me that you love me. Or, Sarah, look at me. This isn't about Emerson. Yes, he needs to change, but this is about you coming across respectfully as your way of showing your reverence for Me.

To seal this idea, I use one of the most memorable images of the entire conference. Whatever you do by way of love or respect, you do not do it primarily to get your marriage off *the Crazy Cycle*. Nor do you do it to get your spouse to meet your needs. Ultimately, to practice love or respect, especially in moments of tension or conflict, you look at your spouse and just over his or her shoulder you envision Jesus Christ, standing there looking at you, saying, *Truly, as you have done it to your spouse, you have done it unto Me!*

As I tell the crowd, "When I see Jesus back there behind Sarah, it's as if I hear Him saying, Emerson, this isn't about Sarah, this is about you and Me. Yes, I see her finger in your face as she scolds you for being unloving. Yes, I agree she could be more respectful. So what will you do? Just walk away, or look beyond her to Me because, as a man of honor, you will do the loving thing as unto Me?"

I get letter after letter about the Christ-over-the-shoulder image. Here's an example: "If I see Jesus looking at me over my husband's shoulder, then I'm bound to treat my husband with the respect due to him out of my love and reverence for Jesus. I do believe that was the single brightest lightbulb flash for me!"

To realize you are doing your marriage as unto Christ is revolutionizing—and sobering. The image of Christ standing there, just beyond your spouse's shoulder as part of every conversation, is a reminder that you will be standing before Him at the final judgment. As you envision Him, you will more fully understand that your marriage is really a tool and a test to deepen and demonstrate your love and your reverence for your Lord. You will grasp the power of *the Rewarded Cycle*:

HIS LOVE BLESSES REGARDLESS OF HER RESPECT

HER RESPECT BLESSES REGARDLESS OF HIS LOVE

Prayer: Thank the Lord for being the "seen" guest in every conversation you have together. Pray for the strength and wisdom to always envision Him at the center of your marriage, especially in moments of tension or conflict.

Action: As you talk together, each of you can practice seeing Christ over each other's shoulder. Talk about how this feels. What is the Lord telling you?

For more "husband-friendly devotionals that wives truly love," see Emerson's book The Love & Respect Experience (Thomas Nelson, 2011).

A Personal Word: "In God We Trust"

I need God. You need God. So, here is what you can do if you are feeling a bit helpless and hopeless. It is amazing to me the number of people who think about praying but never really pray.

The Bible says, "You have not because you ask not" (James 4:2). We're not talking about health and wealth. We are talking about you asking God to enable you to show love and respect at those times you don't want to or feel unable to. I am telling you, if anything is heard in heaven, it is this prayer. This is an unselfish prayer. This is a prayer based on the heart of God.

Too many pray, "God here is what is on my heart. Please fulfill my desires for me." That is totally different from praying, "God here is what is on Your heart. Please fulfill Your desires for me."

Ephesians 5:33 is the will of God, is it not? John the Apostle said, "And this is the confidence which we have before Him, if we ask anything according to His will, He hears us. And if we know that He hears us in whatever we ask, we know that we have the requests which we have asked Him" (1 John 5:14,15).

So, when you have something on your heart that is also on God's heart, look out! When your will is in keeping with His will, He hears you.

Husbands, it is God's will that you love. Ask Him for help.

Wives, it is God's will that you respect. Ask Him for help.

Heaven responds. God is not some cosmic killjoy. Trust Him. Pray this prayer over the next several weeks.

Dear Father,

I need you. I cannot love and respect like this. But I know You hear me when I ask You to help me. Forgive me where I have been unloving and disrespectful. I open my heart to You, Father. I will not be fearful nor angry at You or my spouse. I see my partner in a whole new light. I forgive my spouse. I will appreciate my partner as different not wrong. I am actually excited, Lord. Fill my heart with love and reverence for You. Ultimately, this is about You and me. It isn't about my spouse.

Thank You for this enlightenment. My greatest reward comes from doing this "unto" You.

Prepare me this day for those moments of conflict. I especially ask You to put love and respect in my heart when I feel unloved and disrespected. There is no credit for loving and respecting when it is easy. I believe You hear me. I anticipate You responding to me. I have on my heart what is on Your heart. I thank You in advance for helping me take the next step.

I believe You will reward me throughout eternity for what I do in my marriage. I believe an eternal first moment is coming in which I will be overwhelmed. Today, I renew my commitment to believe that everything I do toward my spouse matters to You. Nothing is wasted. When I am loving and respectful during a conflict, this contributes to my eternal reward. Salvation is a free gift through Jesus Christ. I cannot earn this. But rewards come in response to what I do daily in the home. My eye has not seen, my ear has not heard and

it has not entered my heart what You intend to do in response to my love and respect in the home. Thank You for revealing this to me. I am humbled.

I believe this brings conviction to my spouse if anything will, but I don't do it for that reason.

I believe this will influence my children. I am committed to leaving a godly legacy.

I believe this matures me and reveals my freedom of spirit. My marriage is a test and tool.

And I believe this touches Your heart as I do this "unto You." I do this out of love and reverence for You because You love me and intend to glorify me throughout eternity. It's between You and me. I am a true believer.

In Your Name, Amen.

Answer Key

Session 1

- love
- respect
- love
- respect
- men
- women
- unloved
- disrespected

Session 2

- men
- women
- unloved
- disrespected
- unloved
- disrespected

Session 3

- love
- respect
- respect
- love
- Face to Face
- Mad
- Empathize
- Resolve/Reconcile
- Committed
- Treasure
- Closeness -- Face to Face

Session 4

- Openness -- Mad
- Understanding -- Empathize
- Peacemaking -- Resolve/Reconcile
- Loyalty -- Committed
- Esteem -- Treasure

Session 5

- Work & Achieve
- Protect & Provide
- Strong & Lead & Decisions
- Analyze & Counsel
- Friendship
- Sexual
- Conquest -- Work & Achieve

Session 6

- Heirarchy -- Protect & Provide
- Authority -- Strong & Lead
- Insight -- Analyze & Counsel
- Relationship -- Friendship
- Sexuality -- Sexual

Session 9

- Moment
- Unto

Session 10

- Maturity
- Response